W9-DCF-858

MEMOS
TO THE
PRIME
MINISTER

What Canada Could Be in the 21st Century

HARVEY SCHACHTER, EDITOR
FOREWORD BY HENRY MINTZBERG

JOHN WILEY & SONS

TORONTO • NEW YORK • CHICHESTER • WEINHEIM • BRISBANE • SINGAPORE

John Wiley & Sons Canada, Ltd.
22 Worcester Road
Etobicoke, Ontario
M9W 1L1

National Library of Canada Cataloguing in Publication Data

Main entry under title:
  Memos to the Prime Minister : what Canada could be in the 21st century

ISBN 0-471-64649-0

  1. Canada—Politics and government—1993- 2. Canada—Economic policy—1991- 3. Canada—Social policy. I. Schachter, Harvey

FC635.M45 2001   971.064'8   C2001-901566-6
F1034.2.MY5 2001

Production Credits
Cover Design and Text: Interrobang Graphic Design Inc.
Printing and Binding: Tri-Graphic Printing Limited

Printed and bound in Canada
10 9 8 7 6 5 4 3 2 1

CONTENTS

FOREWORD

Time for Canada?

Henry Mintzberg

O n February 21, 1905, Prime Minister Wilfrid Laurier remarked in the House of Commons that "the twentieth century could be the century of Canada." Famous words, apparently wrong. Or were they just premature? Maybe the twenty-first century could be that of Canada—if we have the courage to follow our natural instincts. Canada has something special to offer this strange world, at this strange juncture: America with the edge off.

America, the United States so called, has offered a great deal to the world: a lifestyle of openness, energy, and innovation, together with substantial wealth. But that has come with some unpleasant baggage that is increasingly unpleasant these days: a certain angst, the insecurity of excessive mobility, individualism and self-interest carried to extremes.

Now the world is grabbing it all, with a vengeance. People everywhere, it seems, wish to become more American, or more "global" (which is the same thing). That is a process we as Canadians understand well, because we have lived it longer and more concertedly than anyone else. So while continuing to grab some of it, and having to deal with those who wish to grab all of it, most of us have developed a certain cynicism toward it too. That can make us pretentious, but it has also bred a healthy skepticism that helped us chart another course.

We Canadians love to distinguish ourselves from Americans. It is a sport in the country well ahead of hockey (indeed, it carries into hockey). We sit in our maple trees like panthers, waiting to pounce on any difference that goes by. Somehow that makes us feel less threatened by it all.

I once got into a cab in the north of England and was promptly told by the driver that he was *not* English. "I am a Yorkshireman," he proclaimed. Go explain that to a visiting bushman from Papua New Guinea, I wanted to tell him. Likewise for us in Canada. And yet, these days especially, I believe the differences that exist do matter. That edge being off is important. It can allow Canada to become a model to the world.

Why is it that year after year Canada ranks so high—and so often—in those United Nations surveys of quality of life? I have a neighbour in Prague (where I am spending some time now) who used to work for Statistics Canada and ended up running the Statistical Institute there. He laughs whenever I talk about this. Sure, he says, Canadians designed the instrument so Canada should come first. But he has it wrong; that is more like an American perspective. The Canadian perspective is that Canada comes so high *despite* the fact that Canadians designed the instrument. That is one of the key little differences. As a colleague once remarked, Americans say, "Hey! Get off my car!" Canadians say, "Get off my car… eh?"

I think we come out so high on these surveys because, leaving the weather aside, we have it both ways: almost all the wealth and openness of America without a number of its most pressing problems.

History has put us in a different place: in North America, without being quite American. With a different territory has come a different past—no revolution, no slavery, a long thin country dependent on the intervention of government instead of a great big rectangle responsive to individual initiative. We also inherited, or at least retained, a system of government that challenges its leadership at every turn—in Parliament and on television—rather than placing it on a pedestal from which it must inevitably fall. So we don't much believe in heroic leadership in this country, which in my opinion is one of the major problems now plaguing the United States, in business no less than in government.

From these and other historical differences, we diverged from America along a number of other important lines. For one, we actually believe in government. When a Canadian says, "Somebody should do something about that," he or she almost inevitably means government. Not least of the things we expect from government is protection, for everyone, including the disadvantaged. Sure governments in Canada have gone overboard on some of this, as in an unemployment insurance system that was so easily manipulated, just as they have erred on the other side more recently by excessive cuts in medicare. But it is a sign of the times that we are supposed to apologize for our generosity while elevating selfishness to some sort of high calling. Thank goodness we have retained much of that generosity.

The Tolerant Society

If Americans relish individuality, we favour tolerance. That word, to my mind, captures Canada best. We are a tolerant society in a world becoming increasingly mercenary. Call that meek, if you wish, so long as you realize that meek may not be a bad thing in a nasty world. We pay a price for this—what other country on earth allows an independence movement to set the question, hold the referendum, and count the ballots?—but it also translates into a certain respect for each other. That makes this country a rather comfortable place to live in a world increasingly prone to discomfort.

Tolerance is perhaps most clearly manifested in our role as international peacekeepers. Evident exceptions notwithstanding, we take to that role rather naturally, and perform the job rather well. Being in between, blaming no one, seems to be in our genes. Americans go into that role and all too often act like cowboys in search of some Indians.

I also see this characteristic in my own field of management. I once ran a Canadian Deans Panel at an international conference. Present were the deans of the Harvard, Stanford, and London Business Schools, all Canadians. Perhaps this was a coincidence, but I chose to see it in relation to that Canadian characteristic. Maybe as a tolerant low-key people, we tend to produce leaders who manage quietly instead of heroically. (Incidentally, as I was developing these ideas some years ago, I came across an article by colleagues at École des Hautes Études Commerciales, the large francophone business school in Montreal, who described leadership in Quebec in rather similar ways.)

Maybe business school professors prefer quiet leadership. Indeed, maybe "knowledge workers" in general do, because Canada seems to do well in that sphere. We have by far the most collegial universities I have ever come across; we are especially strong in the field of consulting engineering services, and we have a health care system that, to paraphrase Churchill's quote, may be the worst in the world except for all the alternatives. We may not be able to run trucking companies worth a damn—that is what a chief executive of CP once told me—because that takes tough cookies, but we seem to do fine with professionals. Maybe we should let the Americans run our trucking companies while they let us run their health care!

Here is how the man who built up Bombardier, Laurent Beaudoin, described that company's management style, in *The McKinsey Quarterly* in 1997: "We are very Canadian in the way we handle acquisitions. We hardly ever lay people off. Experience has shown that if we treat them well and give them the right opportunities to grow, they will be productive and create jobs for others."

Meg Graham, a colleague at McGill, likes to talk about the St. Lawrence Valley, from Quebec City through Montreal to Ottawa. Not exactly Silicon Valley, she believes, but something built by people with a different lifestyle. Perhaps that takes the edge off, just a little bit, so that they can manage a little more quietly. I don't know if that is true, but I do know one thing: It could be true if we have the courage to recognize such differences and make something of it.

All the characteristics mentioned above are obviously not ours alone. They can be found in the United States and everywhere else. The difference is that while America tilts away from them, drawing others along, Canada remains where it has long been, with a tilt toward them. And that makes all the difference. It brings me to what may be the most important characteristic of all in this country: balance.

A Triumph of Balance

The world is fast going out of balance now, to the right, much as the states of central and Eastern Europe earlier went out of balance to the left. The reason, I believe, is the assumption that "capitalism has triumphed."

This belief is both fallacious and dangerous. Capitalism never triumphed at all. Balance triumphed. While the communist states were utterly out of balance, with so much power in the hands of the state, those of the West—Canada not least, but the United States and many others—balanced strong government with solid markets and a vigorous social sector in between. But now, failing to understand this, people everywhere are in the process of emasculating their governments while allowing their social institutions to be captured by market forces and corporatist attitudes.

Capitalism is not good because communism was bad. Rampant individualism is no better than uncontrolled collectivism; "free enterprise" is no less an aberration than "democracy of the proletariat." What matters is free people—free to be our individual and collective selves, free of the dogmas foisted on us by myopic economists and the insatiable rich.

We manage to retain some semblance of balance in Canada. It seems to be intrinsic to our nature. We believe in capitalism alongside strong government. We provide opportunity together with protection. We are a country in which much of the population herds just to the left of centre. Some other countries swing between left and right, from one extreme to another. We stay in the same place.

America does not swing. It has been moving steadily to the right for years, more slowly under Democrats, more quickly under Republicans. Britain has been doing much the same thing, albeit for a time in the name of some mysterious "third way." Canada, in contrast, does offer another way, and it is not particularly mysterious. In a world of excess, we somehow maintain balance.

All of this may sound self-satisfied—we have that inclination in Canada too, at least when we compare ourselves with the Americans. But far stronger is our inclination to self-depre-cate. And so a little recognition of what is good in this country — or, should I say, what we should realize as good—is hardly out of order, especially in a world that needs more tolerance, more comfort, more generosity, and especially greater balance.

Courage of Our Convictions?

Examples of where we have failed to follow national instincts are instructive. Fifteen years ago, we had legislation that required pharmaceutical companies to license patented med-icines to generic producers at moderate fees. The pharmaceu-tical industry was threatened by this—worried that other countries might follow—and so mounted an aggressive cam-paign to have it rescinded. Eventually a Canadian government acquiesced. Now that same pharmaceutical industry, in a supreme act of arrogance, challenged an African country in its own courts to stop it from importing AIDS medicines from generic producers at a small fraction of that industry's price. The intellectual "property" of these companies had to be pro-tected at any cost in human misery—and at any price they cared to set. Capitalism finally triumphed. We had it right in Canada years ago; we just didn't have the courage to stay the course.

Another example concerns advertising. Thirty years ago, a federal minister, worried about deception, proposed legislation that would have subjected certain advertising to a credibility screening by a lay panel. It was laughed out of Parliament—at least by the vested interests. So uncontrolled advertising continues to demean us. Freedom of individual expression, including the freedom of corporations to speak as if they were individual people, remains unchallenged by freedom *from* expression: the right to privacy, to peace and quiet in public places. I believe we had that one right too, if only we had the courage to see it through.

Imagine if the governments of Saskatchewan and Canada had backed down on medicare, in the face of pressures from the United States not unlike those mounted against that pharmaceutical legislation. Imagine further if medicare were instead being proposed today. Now that would be laughable—state funding for almost all health care! Unthinkable in today's world. Instead, we do have medicare, which despite its problems remains immensely popular in this country. The unthinkable becomes natural when people have the foresight and the courage to make it happen. "All change seems impossible," wrote the French philosopher Alain, "but once accomplished, it is the state you are no longer in that seems impossible."

All of this is to conclude what I am calling our national instincts are not bad, eh? Indeed, they are often rather good, especially when juxtaposed against the world we now live in. We get into trouble when we deny them, when we are afraid to go our own way. What makes Canada such a pleasant place to live is not just that it is so overtly like the United States, but that it is so covertly unlike it.

When the world was flat, location mattered. You had to be in the centre of things—in Athens, or London, or New York. In this respect, the world remained flat long after Columbus sailed. Only recently, with the development of communications technology, has the world become round. Moose Jaw is now as good as New York, if you are hooked up. There is no centre on a sphere. The centre becomes wherever people do what is needed; they draw the attention of others and thus become the hub of a network. Well then, as a model for society in the twenty-first century, why not Canada?

A Mexican diplomat reportedly quipped that while Mexico is a problem looking for a solution, Canada is a solution looking for a problem. The world has a problem. Canada offers a solution. If we have the courage to be ourselves, if we have the confidence to follow our national instincts, this can be the century of Canada. Quietly.

POLITICS AND POLICY IN A CHANNEL-CLICKER AGE

Harvey Schachter

A t 8:57 p.m., I clicked my television remote, and the five federal party leaders dissolved and disappeared into the blackness. I felt both saddened and energized. Saddened because I am a fan of political debates, and while I had looked to the November 2000 clash as a chance to better understand the options facing this country, the leaders had let me down, preferring pithy billboard statements that insulted my intelligence rather than grappling with ideas. But I was energized, because I had escaped: The channel clicker had empowered me.

How much the public is interested in politics and policy is actually a subject itself of stimulating debate. The early studies of political behaviour in the 1940s in the United States found voters had a startling inability to distinguish between the policies of presidential candidates—even the main elements of their platforms. Although we live in what seems a more politically literate age, with the leaders entering our living room many nights on the television news, Richard Johnston, the UBC political scientist who led many of the academic teams that carried out in-depth studies of Canadian elections in the past two decades and who is just completing a similar, pioneering study of the last American election, suggests that there is no reason to believe that the average citizen is any better informed these days. As a newspaper editor, I used to be amazed at the confusion on political issues even among people who chose to write letters to the editor. At the same time, many people have a breathtaking knowledge of politics and political issues.

For all of us—whichever of those camps we fall into—there has been a seismic shift in the past decade and a half, as we try to grapple with issues that seem increasingly complex. You don't have to be interested in political issues to know our health care system is under strain, or to be frightened by Walkerton, or to wonder about our ability as a nation to keep up with our powerful neighbour to the south let alone to remain a single nation. It's easy to feel overwhelmed by those issues, whatever your interest in politics and your base of knowledge.

That's why when election debates take place, people tune in. The more those issues trouble us, the more we seek new answers. But the channel clicker that allowed me to make the political leaders vanish has become the symbol of our political age. In the same way as we flip from channel to channel looking for better entertainment, we flip from political leader to leader and desperately hunt for fresh policy options in a frantic effort to spice up our political life. Our search for novelty applies to politics as it does to other forms of entertainment. We tire easily; nothing seems to satisfy us for long.

The Old and the New

There have been some long-serving political leaders in the modern era, Jean Chrétien and Ralph Klein among them. Joe Clark continues to plod along, our political Energizer bunny. But there still seems to be a yearning, overall, for new faces, although our political system—with its regional divisions and closed shop in picking party leaders—seems to prevent us from fully acting on this impulse. The declining turnout in elections is probably a manifestation of those cross-pressures between wanting change and recognizing it isn't really available.

You can see this phenomenon better with the American presidency, which is more of a fashion show for ideas and personality, and which in the TV era has stopped being a sure thing for an incumbent to win in re-election bids. Ronald Reagan and Bill Clinton have to be viewed as exceptions in the age of the channel clicker for being able to gain re-election, something that in the past was fairly automatic.

Most of our political ideas in this channel-clicker age aren't really new, even if that is what we are obsessed with finding. They are all derived from political thought that traces back at least a few centuries. Adam Smith, after all, seems more popular and influential today than in his own era. Communitarian notions, similarly, have a long history. Pharmacare is just medicare extended to another area of health where limited individual finances can prevent people from obtaining proper care. The new and old intermingle. Even feminism, the political philosophy that probably had the most profound impact on us in the last 30 years, harkens back a long way. Although there are new applications to those older thoughts, the reality is that political policy tends to be like *Star Trek* reruns—ever present and overly familiar.

Those who expect fresh visions from political leaders run up against that stumbling block. It is hard to come up with something new and invigorating. Even if a politician could develop a new vision and start to sell it, the vision would become old very soon—probably on the second day of the news cycle. Look at how quickly Stockwell Day went from being something fresh to something tiresome. Beyond that, in an age of dissent and declining deference to political leaders, vision gets trashed— and mocked—very quickly. Donna Dasko, senior vice-president of Environics Research group, is startled by what she sees in recent years in the focus groups she supervises across the country: "Invariably people are skeptical. Nobody is enthusiastic. People look at politics with a jaundiced eye. A political leader today doesn't get the respect you did a few decades ago."

Promoting a vision may work in business. No CEO today can admit to not having a vision for his or her company. But a CEO has the command of followers that a political leader can only envy. Employees go along, or leave (or stay very silent, waiting until the CEO's departure). No CEO has a leader of the

Opposition, with the right to ask tough, insulting questions daily while the media captures and rebroadcasts the sparring. And no CEO has to face the soul-destroying slowness of Parliament in grappling with new visions, strategies, and policies. CEOs implement with channel-clicker speed. Public life, however, requires policies to be thoroughly studied and debated—and then studied and debated yet again. Tom Peters, who celebrates fast-paced, dramatic CEOs and organizations, says that is he plans an addition on his house he expects his municipality to approve it immediately, but if his neighbour wants an addition it should face a lengthy study. It's no wonder the "vision thing" is in such short supply in politics.

A Search for Understanding

That being said, as I met just after the election debate with Karen Milner and Rob Dawson—the two people from John Wiley & Sons who spearheaded this book—we sensed that many Canadians were genuinely searching for understanding about social, economic, and political issues but were deeply disenchanted that our politicians and our political system were letting them down. To answer that need, we set out to gather some prominent Canadians who could educate and inspire us, setting out their ideas in memos to the prime minister.

Those memos are *individual* agendas. There was no attempt to develop a comprehensive agenda—or indeed to touch on all the important issues facing us. We chose to concentrate on leadership, the economy, technology, social services, health care, the environment, and matters of regionalism and Quebec's role in Canada. We also chose to solicit varying views—including on two of the issues that were considered too explosive for even proponents to discuss in the last election, two-tiered health care and a flat tax. Nobody would subscribe to all the ideas advanced in this book (indeed, I would worry about anybody who did). And many of the contributors will be repulsed by the essays gathered alongside theirs.

The memos are divided into four sections, to make it easier for readers: Leading Canada, Economic Canada, Social Canada, and Constitutional Canada. But most of them inevitably roam beyond the section in which they are placed. As the project developed steam, friends and contributors were always quick to suggest other possible writers who we could include. But we began, unfortunately, with a practical limit of about thirty, and I chose, rightly or wrongly, to avoid some obvious contenders who I felt were overexposed, their ideas and policies already well known from other venues. I gathered some people who are quite well known and others who are not broadly familiar but are nevertheless leading experts in their field. There's even a writer of detective novels for a change of pace. In a channel-clicker era, I wanted contributors who could not only educate but also to some extent surprise.

Our choice for the foreword, for example, was Henry Mintzberg, the iconoclast McGill professor who has a fascination with management and governance in both business and public life, relishes debunking pretence and established notions, and who from his twin perches in the Laurentians and Europe can see Canada a bit differently from the rest of us. His essay revolves around what is special about Canada and Canadians, and how that can improve the world.

We urged writers to offer prescriptions, not descriptions. Too many commentaries of this sort tend to devote 80% to 90% of the space to descriptions of what is wrong with the current situation and, at best, at the end throw out a hint of what the solution might be. We wanted to reverse that. While not being formulaic—each essay had its own needs—we wanted to start with the assumption that readers are familiar with the issues being discussed, have a sense of the problems, and are seeking answers, so the essay could theoretically focus 80% to 90% of its attention on the proposed solution. That was probably more philosophical than practical—you have to examine the past to understand the future—but you will find the emphasis inside is on prescriptions.

LEADING
CANADA

Hugh Segal

Matthew Mendelsohn

Donald J. Savoie

Sheelagh Whittaker

*David Conklin and
Mary Crossan*

Part One

Hugh Segal

Hugh Segal *is president of the Institute for Research on Public Policy,* Canada's oldest, nonpartisan think tank. Mr. Segal has held a series of senior positions in the public and private sector, including chief of staff to the prime minister, associate secretary of cabinet for federal-provincial relations in Ontario, corporate affairs and industrial relations vice-president at John Labatt Ltd., and chairman of the TACT group of companies. A long-time Progressive Conservative party strategist, he was first ballot runner-up in the party's federal leadership race in 1998. Mr. Segal is a professor of public policy at the School of Business at Queen's University and senior fellow at the university's School of Policy Studies. A graduate of the University of Ottawa, he has written three books on politics and public policy: *No Surrender, Beyond Greed,* and *In Defence of Civility.*

MEMORANDUM

To: **The Prime Minister of Canada**

From: **Hugh Segal** | *President,*
The Institute for Research
in Public Policy

Subject: **Leading, Not Following**

We Canadians are a hard lot to lead—especially in peacetime, although history tells us that we aren't all that much easier to lead in times of war. But we can be inspired and we do respond to leadership when it is rooted in the realities of the Canadian soul and the fabric of our hopes and aspirations.

Appealing to our fears may be politically adept and sometimes even clever—but it is a short-haul game. Many of the merchants of populism appeal to the most fearful, narrow-minded, and short-sighted among us. While we have no more of those types than any other country, and I would argue probably substantially fewer as a percentage of the whole population than most, they have been known to cluster and become a powerful force for inertia, or worse.

The desire as prime minister to play things safe and avoid the risks of spending political capital must at times be overwhelming. I urge you to resist it. The ability to really lead is immeasurably enhanced when Canadians decide that a prime minister is prepared to lead even if it costs re-election. It's funny how those kinds of prime ministers—Trudeau, Mulroney, et

INSTITUTE FOR RESEARCH ON PUBLIC POLICY

INSTITUT DE RECHERCHE EN POLITIQUES PUBLIQUES

1470 Peel
Suite 200
Montréal, Québec
H3A 1T1
(514) 985-2461
Fax: (514) 985-2559
E-mail/Courriel
irpp@irpp.org
Website/Internet
www.irpp.org

al—do get re-elected despite singular controversies during their terms of office. And they did not need four opposition parties to divide the anti-government vote to do it.

The ability to build trust and inspire has two sides. The first is personal honesty and frankness. The second relates to the substance of the leadership itself. The personal honesty and frankness bit is new in Canadian politics—a product of the proximity to the prime minister that the modern media provides to the public. In the past, the aloof, all-knowing, all-powerful leader was the Canadian norm—sort of an Anglo-Saxon and Charlemagne-like fable rolled into a detached omnipotent great one. Most Canadians have little time for that approach any more, yet some leaders in recent times inherited this silliness from their mentors of many years ago.

Today, a leader should be frank about what she or he knows—or knows not. A prime minister should not be afraid to be vulnerable or human. Admitting a mistake or confessing to uncertainty in difficult areas is not a sign of weakness but a sign of strength. We heard recently of a prime minister who was alleged to have broken down and cried in his caucus because of the risk that the country could be lost in a Quebec referendum. I don't know if it's true—but had he broken down in public, the sheer integrity and sincerity of that emotion would have endeared him to many Canadians who disagreed with his approach to the issue, let alone those who agreed.

Rigidity in defence of narrow-mindedness is no virtue; flexibility in support of a genuine set of goals is no vice. And while our parliamentary system is adversarial, a prime minister need not be.

There will be issues where division is truly unavoidable. But they need not be outnumbered by issues where division is manufactured—a good rule to remember, for both a prime minister and his or her civil servants, and political co-partisans. Party labels should be badges of honour and principled bridges to the unaligned and the temporary coalitions that will be forged on compelling issues of the day. They should not be blinkers from the sun or soundproof insulation keeping out the voices and concerns of honest dissent.

The substance of leadership counts along with the style. Style can get in the way of substance—a problem that will cost dearly. But that cost pales by comparison to what is exacted by the voters when style is used to mask the absolute absence of substance. When the black hole of nothingness becomes apparent, voters wreak havoc with the revenge they take—and who can blame them?

The Two Extremes of Leadership

There are two extremes in leadership styles—the judgemental and the deliberative. The judgemental has no specific agenda, deals with issues as they come, and tries to be fair and pragmatic. The deliberative has a clear and deliberate program, and plans and works daily—even hourly—to support the precepts of that plan. Many a judgemental leader has been called passive and disengaged. Many a deliberative leader has been called arrogant and insensitive. The leadership answer is not at the extremes but in the mix that is shaped by each leader in his or her own way and time.

Let me make the case respectfully that the nature of the Canadian soul and aspirations invites a leader with a broad vision on direction and purpose, as well as deeply sunk roots on how and at what pace we proceed as a country in support of that vision. We are a mix of descendants from some fascinating people: First Nations that were fiercely independent and proud; French Canadians deserted by their motherland but determined to maintain language, culture, and civilization; British and American families that rejected American republicanism and England's class structure; Scots and Irish who sought freedom from hunger and persecution; Eastern Europeans who chose freedom, good farmland, and religious tolerance relative to the poverty and bigotry at home; Italians, Portuguese, and other southern Europeans who brought strong family and industrious values; South Asian and Oriental Canadians who chose economic opportunity and freedom; Americans in the west who came for cheap grazing land and opportunity. All voted with their heart and feet to build Canada and their own lives and fortunes (although not necessarily in that order, of course).

Our ancestors all had different questions shaped by their history and circumstance—but for all, Canada was the only and the best answer. None has been prepared to surrender who they were in support of who we all are. All have strong views on who we should be and how we should govern ourselves. Those views do differ in significant ways—and playing on those differences plus the regional overlay that underlines them is the political candy of our time. Some who have been prime minister have been ready to exploit and fan those differences. The real challenge is to sink the foundations of genuine leadership into the rich soil of what unites and binds.

Impossible you say? Let's see.

I venture that many of the sovereignists in Quebec who want Canada to be radically reshaped as a two-nation federation of equals would share an Alberta small businessman's concern about government that is too large or overbearing at the federal or provincial level. Many of the fishing families in Newfoundland who worry about their future share the southern Ontario interest in clean water and solid health care. Many of the pensioners in northern New Brunswick who want access to the best medical services possible share that interest with retirees in the Okanagan Valley. And the values of decency, fairness, avoiding waste, respect for diversity, and encouraging young people to excel would be universal. Those are the key elements that form the soil in which the roots of leadership can be truly and genuinely set.

A Time for Elevation

Let me also suggest that Canadians respond well to a mixture of both breadth and depth. In other words, one doesn't want the expression of leadership to be, like a flat prairie, all horizon and no elevation. Leadership is having the courage to set a goal that society is not quite ready for but in a way that invites everyone to help attain it in their own way. It may be impossible to eradicate poverty, but it is never wrong to try. It may be difficult to accept all those who want to come to Canada legally, but it would be a mistake not to look for ways to accept as many as possible. It may be risky to seek new international standards on the environment or fiscal prudence, but it is even riskier not to try.

There is a difference between hectoring the public and promoting public debate and discussion. There is a difference between imposing a vision, and leading and shaping a collective sense of will and opportunity.

The calendar renders the new millennium no more special than any other threshold of time or place—but the conditions under which we enter the millennium do. It is time for a prime minister to lay out a path that places the necessary integration with a North American common market in the right balance with the sovereignty and independence we need as Canadians to preserve what we care about at home and abroad. It is time for a prime minister to share a vision of how we achieve both economic growth and social progress—and what choices we must face to carry it off. It is time for a prime minister to tell us Canada's view of the world: how our interests on this continent can be protected, pursued, and expressed through diplomatic and military strength. It is time for a prime minister to tell us how Confederation can adapt to a changing world and the evolving aspirations of Canadians in both the west and the east. It is time for a prime minister to describe the real costs of environmental degradation and begin building consensus between producers and consumers of energy on the sane way ahead. It is time for a prime minister to define Canada's world stance on the critical foreign policy questions that will define the world we share and the prospects for Canada and her allies in that world.

Wherever a leader is in his or her mandate, every prime minister must surely answer key questions every step of the way:

- Aside from my own personal victory—which was an instrument, not a goal—what did I come to the Prime Minister's Office to change, to reverse, or to improve?
- What are the key policy changes I can make at my point in the mandate that others before or after will be unable to do?
- What are the glaring challenges facing Canada that if left unaddressed will seriously damage the prospects of our kids in the years ahead?

Prime ministerial leadership requires asking those questions on a regular basis and updating the answers quite systematically. And when a priority for leadership is found and embraced, it is wrong to formulate one's approach and then deliver oneself of it in a way that implies that the problem has been diagnosed, the prescription has been found, and the all-knowing prime minister or government of the day will now proceed—expecting a mix of hosannas, applause, and compliance. Leadership is about shaping the public mood with frank talk, honest explanation, and the art of honourable persuasion. Convincing one's caucus, cabinet, and party is a good beginning—but just a beginning.

The Canadian public will be skeptical and cynical—and that's a good thing. But as we have seen during the Gulf War and during the anti-deficit policies of the mid-1990s, Canadians will respond when a case is logical, honourably made, and legitimately advanced. Inspiration comes from the sincerity of the proponent and the integrity of the proposition advanced. Expertise is important as an instrument within the broad context of leadership—but it is in and of itself not sufficient. Canadians will not care how much you know until they know how much you care.

In the end, Prime Minister, leadership is not about your needs but ours, not about your career but about the careers of Canadians that you help build and advance. In the end, the sincerity and empathy that form the soft core of any strength and determination are fundamental to the leadership that Canadians have the right to expect from their prime minister.

Matthew Mendelsohn

Matthew Mendelsohn | *is associate professor in the Department of Political Studies and director of the Canadian Public Opinion Archive at Queen's University.* He served as senior advisor in the Privy Council Office from 1996 to 1998, where he directed the polling unit for Intergovernmental Affairs. He has published extensively on the media, elections, public opinion, public consultations, referendums, and Canadian and Quebec politics. He currently advises several government departments on polling and public consultations, and is one of the architects of the annual tracking survey "Portraits of Canada" conducted by the Centre for Research and Information on Canada. He received his B.A. from McGill and Ph.D. from the Université de Montréal.

DEPARTMENT OF POLITICAL STUDIES

Mackintosh-Corry Hall, Room c321
Queen's University
Kingston, Ontario, Canada K7L 3N6
Tel 613 533-6230
Fax 613 533-6848
http://politics.queensu.ca/politics/

MEMORANDUM

To: **The Prime Minister of Canada**

From: **Matthew Mendelsohn** | *Professor of Political Science, Queen's University*

Subject: **Healing Social, Political, and Regional Divisions**

Over the past three decades, the Liberal Party of Canada has drifted away from its most important historic mission: finding consensus between regional and linguistic groups and building broad national coalitions that ensured many different groups had a voice in government. The Chrétien Liberals—even more so than the Trudeau Liberals—have been successful at the Liberals' other historic mission: vacuuming up votes and winning elections. But the majorities of Laurier, Mackenzie King, and St. Laurent not only kept the Liberals in power, but also fulfilled an essential national purpose by building national coalitions that worked to overcome and accommodate various regional conflicts. The same was true of the Tory majority coalitions. They were about more than just keeping the winners in power; they were also about finding ways to manage the centrifugal forces in the country. This earned both the label "brokerage parties," because they worked to broker the diffuse interests and beliefs of different linguistic, regional, and national groups by giving them all a voice in government, instead of acting as ideological parties or class parties defending the interests of one or two groups.

Recent majority governments, however, have not served the purpose of moderating conflict and attenuating dissensus. The Liberal Party since 1968 has satisfied its own ends by continuing to win elections but has stopped serving the broader public function that it used to fulfil. Because of the Liberals' refusal to find accommodation with some of the most important movements for change in the country—western devolutionists, populists, and Quebec nationalists—they now actually exacerbate rather than moderate regional and linguistic differences.

At our current juncture, for Canada to work, the Liberal Party must work. Narrowly constructed majorities on a thin electoral base are sufficient to win elections in a fractured system, but nothing more. Through a number of small and quite feasible changes to the way in which the public is involved in decision-making, the accommodation of conflict necessary to Canada's smooth functioning could be re-instilled. This task, however, requires greater public participation because parties cannot do it alone. In the 1940s or 1950s, as long as every group felt that it was represented around the cabinet table, most citizens felt that their interests had been adequately defended. Now, citizens are less willing to defer to compromises negotiated by elites behind closed doors. In order to build new national consensus, the public must be re-engaged with politics.

The Four Sources of Political Cleavages

There have traditionally been four potential sources of ideological conflict in Canada: economic, social, divisions over definitions of the Canadian nation, and divisions over democracy itself.

The economic factor—how much should one restrain the market or how generous social programs should be—has played a role in every Canadian election. The social element has been more sporadically involved, in the form of abortion rights or, in an earlier time, prohibition of alcohol. That conflict generally pits traditional and sometimes authoritarian values with little tolerance of social deviance against a more libertarian, secular, socially liberal set of values.

On defining the Canadian nation, there have been intense conflicts concerning the role of the federal government in relation to the provinces —is the federal government a superior order of government?—as well as intense conflicts regarding the place of accommodation itself: Is Canada multinational; is Quebec a distinct society; is Canada a community of communities; must we constantly work toward compromise and consensus?

With regard to the definition of democracy, first the Progressives, then the CCF, on occasion the NDP, and more recently the Alliance, have all made public participation in decision-making a key issue. All those parties appealed to innate populism—particularly in the Canadian west and non-urban centres—and rejected some of the principles of party government in favour of more popular and delegate democracy where elected politicians follow more closely the expressed wishes of their constituents rather than allowing rule by elites.

It's common to view the Liberal Party today as a national brokerage party, bringing people together. This mistake stems from the fact the party continues to be a centrist party on economic and social questions. It picks and chooses from debt reduction, tax relief, and investments in social programs to satisfy simultaneously the left and right of the party, and, although clearly on the secular side of the spectrum on social issues, it has reflected rather than led public opinion by adopting the position of the vast majority of voters on questions such as abortion, same-sex marriage, and euthanasia.

Its centrism on those issues has meant that the Liberal Party's polarization and ideological approach to the other two questions has gone less noticed. It has become an intensely ideological party, at one end of the spectrum on the definition of the Canadian nation and on the question of public participation in decision-making.

The Liberal Party is *the* party of elitist democracy, intensely rejecting calls for greater public participation in decision-making, calls that reflect the evolution in Canadians' values and abilities. While other parties support institutional reform to a greater or lesser extent—more referendums, electoral reform, greater independence for the MP, popular selection of party leaders—the Liberals are derisive of attempts to include the public in decision-making. And public opinion surveys show that Canadians with little trust in "the people" are far more likely to vote Liberal.

On questions related to federalism and Quebec, the Liberal Party has been *the* party of undifferentiated equality—arguing all provinces must be treated in exactly the same manner—and for a strong central government. On the question of equality, the Liberals of the past three decades have refused any recognition of Quebec's national status. The irony is that they have been perfectly prepared to recognize differentiated equality or special status for other communities—aboriginal peoples, linguistic minorities, ethnocultural communities, gender—but their refusal to find any accommodation for Quebec nationalism has been one of the party's defining features in that period.

Likewise, the Liberals have been adamant in their refusal to accommodate devolutionist sentiment elsewhere in the country, particularly in the west. The Liberals have not attempted to broker, accommodate, or find consensus. Instead, they have dismissed recognition of Quebec's national status, have defended a top-down style of federalism, and have argued that public participation in decision-making will lead to chaos.

Of course those are all legitimate positions, but the vigour with which the Liberal Party has defended them raises two crucial issues. First, no one is currently fulfilling the important function of brokering conflict between different linguistic and regional groups. And second, in order to understand our present challenges, we must first recognize that the Liberals have ceased to be a brokerage party. They may be centrist on many issues, but on the definition of the nation and the appropriate role of the citizen in decision-making, they are at an extreme end of the spectrum, vigorously defending positions that are equally vigorously opposed by a large number—perhaps a majority—of Canadians. The irony is that on our most pressing collective challenges, our putative brokerage party has chosen to actually oppose compromise and has refused to adapt to evolutions in Canadian values.

The Liberals need to recognize the legitimacy of alternative views and should do what they have done throughout their history: adopt some of the better ideas suggested by others and moderate them so that they appeal to a wide, pan-Canadian coalition. That would allow us to more creatively address many of our most pressing social and economic challenges. By failing to do so—by being content to play out the clock until the next narrow majority government built on the demonization of those with an alternative vision of the country or democracy— the Liberals do serious long-term damage to the country.

Four Initiatives to Consider

Four initiatives suggest themselves. All these proposals are designed to enable citizens to contribute meaningfully to the public debate between elections and animate the public's instinct for accommodation, an instinct that has been discouraged rather than encouraged by leaders during the past decade.

Turnout continues to drop and disengagement with traditional politics continues to increase. At least part of this stems from the fact that Canadian citizens are increasingly capable of participating in political debate, but have no outlet to do so. The notion that election campaigns provide the public with a vehicle for contributing to policy debate is becoming increasingly absurd, and steps must be taken to increase public participation in ways that encourage accommodation.

Canadians' images of themselves—the mosaic, the peace-keeper, the middle power, brokerage parties—construct a picture of a country built around accommodation, compromise, and negotiation. In the past, elite institutions have been necessary for brokerage, yet these institutions are no longer sufficient because Canadians' attitudes have become far less deferential toward elites. Reanimating the spirit of accommodation requires political leaders to modify existing institutions. The creation of new forms of public consultation—processes, spaces, and institutions where members of the public can engage with government officials in deliberation, brokerage, and accommodation—are therefore called for.

First, parliamentary reform that gives greater autonomy to parliamentarians and greater power to parliamentary committees should be undertaken. These committees should be given greater resources to conduct research and evaluate legislation, greater authority to amend legislation, and greater freedom to travel and conduct public hearings across the country. All of that could be accomplished without any change in legislation.

Second, the government should begin to implement the results of its careful study in the late 1990s of new forms of public consultation and citizen engagement that has sat dormant on government shelves. That implementation could include the creation of citizens' committees on important national issues, similar in operation to royal commissions, but with more popular and interest group participation, and less driven by the preparation of exhaustive research materials.

Canada has come close to using such a model with the National Forum on Health. The Saskatchewan government went even further in its Commission on Medicare. Most countries have moved far ahead of Canada in responding to new participatory values by implementing a variety of citizen engagement techniques.

Two recent, on-going experiments come from the British Isles. The Scottish Civic Forum was designed to increase participation by the voluntary sector in discussion of social policy, with a mandate to frame governmental choices in light of the public dialogue. The Irish National Economic and Social Forum includes government members, employers, unions, and groups traditionally left out of the ordinary policy-making process, with the goal of establishing overall policy frameworks related to economic and social policy. While the Scottish Forum feeds into the policy-making process of government but remains apart, the Irish use a partnership model that actually incorporates elected officials in these consultations. Both are part of a broader network of public dialogue and are occasionally called on by government to carry out consultations on particular issues on the government's behalf.

Third, greater use of the referendum is called for, with citizens having the ability to initiate referendum votes, provided that these do not become immediately binding on governments and provided that legislation passed through referendum can still be amended by governments, preserving the Canadian tradition of responsible government. The referendum legislation of New Zealand and some of the northeastern U.S. states, such as Massachusetts, could serve as examples.

Fourth, the federal government should use the opportunity presented by the three-year review of the Social Union Framework Agreement to build a better and more collaborative intergovernmental climate. The agreement was designed to create more collaborative working relationships between Canadian governments. Little progress has been made on this front, however. The statement of principles outlined in the agreement should be carefully studied, and governments should commit themselves to finding better mechanisms for transforming the commitments into real improvements in process, institutions, and the nature of working relationships.

That would include fulfilling the promise for appeal mechanisms for citizens and governments, and formal bodies charged with rendering judgements about intergovernmental disputes. It would also include formally recognizing Quebec's national status and the de facto asymmetry in Canada. Because the agreement makes commitments to intergovernmental collaboration and citizen engagement, I also recommend the establishment of an advisory committee—jointly appointed by both orders of government—that would be responsible for making recommendations on engagement activities, some of which could include delegating authority for difficult decisions to these engagement processes. Canadians are no longer content to await the news from closed-door cabinet meetings to find out whether the federal government is providing more money to provincial governments for health care or has decided instead to pay down the debt or create its own national home care program. The public must have an opportunity to participate more vibrantly in these kinds of decisions, and the social union agreement provides a potential vehicle.

In conclusion, we need to recognize that the "one-size-fits-all" model of federalism, with the federal government as the senior partner, has become obsolete and insufficiently flexible for responding to today's challenges. In the European Union, for example, different countries have different statuses, some sub-regions have their own governments while others do not, and some large cities have expanded authority while other municipalities do not. By claiming that Nova Scotia, Quebec, and B.C. all need access to the same powers, or that Belleville and Port Alberni need the same constitutional status as Toronto or Vancouver, we render ourselves and our governments unable to respond creatively to a rapidly changing world. All orders of Canadian government—federal, provicial, municipal, territorial, and Aboriginal—must work to negotiate administrative agreements that respond to the particular and unique needs of individual provinces, cities, and regions. This may mean a variety of different kinds of asymmetrical arrangements will develop, with no "master blueprint" except a commitment to find things that work for each jurisdiction, with no expectation that these things need to be applied in other jurisdictions. That is the best hope for accomodating the diversity present within the country.

Donald J. Savoie

Donald J. Savoie *who holds the Clément-Cormier chair in economic development at Université de Moncton,* has extensive work experience in both government and academia and is considered a leading expert on the functioning of government, having been honoured for his work by both the Institute of Public Administration of Canada and the Public Policy Forum. He has held senior positions with the government of Canada, including assistant secretary for corporate and public affairs in the Treasury Board and deputy principal of the Canadian Centre for Management Development. He has published thirty-five books, including *Governing from the Centre: The Concentration of Power in Canadian Politics; The Politics of Public Spending in Canada*; and *Thatcher, Reagan, Mulroney: In Search of a New Bureaucracy*. He holds degrees in politics and economics from Université de Moncton, the University of New Brunswick, and Oxford University.

UNIVERSITÉ DE MONCTON
MONCTON,
NOUVEAU-BRUNSWICK
CANADA
E1A 3E9
TÉLÉPHONE   (506) 858-4467
TÉLÉCOPIEUR   (506) 858-4123

INSTITUT CANADIEN DE RECHERCHE SUR LE DÉVELOPPEMENT RÉGIONAL

MEMORANDUM

To: **The Prime Minister of Canada**

From: **Donald J. Savoie** | *Clément-Cormier Chair
in Economic Development,
Université de Moncton*

Subject: **Reshaping National Political Institutions**

Canada's political institutions are in shambles. There is evidence of this everywhere—in the Senate, which few Canadians now take seriously; in the House of Commons, whose operations a number of its members are trying to reform, before the House slips into irrelevance; in cabinet, which has recently been described as a "focus group rather than a decision-making body;" in the Supreme Court, which now is subject to the kind of bashing until recently reserved for politicians and bureaucrats; and in the national civil service, which still remains plagued by morale problems.

Perhaps someone insulated in Ottawa may not fully appreciate the impact of the above and the implications for the country. But people in the regions, particularly in the western provinces and Atlantic Canada, must live with the consequences. Central Canadians should also be concerned with the growing irrelevance of Parliament and with the concentration of political power in the hands of the prime minister and his most trusted advisors, all located in Ottawa. This power is for the most part hidden—and hidden power in the political realm can be dangerous.

The results of the last federal election were revealing on several fronts. Canada remains deeply divided along regional lines. The government did well in Ontario and Atlantic Canada, the two regions that do not have regional parties, although one could argue that the federal Liberal Party is increasingly becoming Ontario's regional party. One can assume that Atlantic Canadians would have sent a different message to Ottawa if they had had their own regional party to turn to.

Quite apart from the regional factor, in 1999 Jocelyne Bourgon, former clerk of the Privy Council and Canada's most senior civil servant, expressed deep concern over the fact that voter participation in the 1997 election was at the lowest level since 1925. Little did she know that voter participation in the 2000 election would be even lower yet.

Transparent, Accessible, and Regionally Sensitive Institutions

What to do? For a start, we urgently need to make our national political institutions much more transparent, accessible, and regionally sensitive.

I accept that the function of Parliament is not to govern, but rather to hold the government to account for its policies and activities. However, it can no longer do this properly and, accordingly, Parliament has become less and less relevant to Canadians and even to officials in Ottawa. A recent survey of federal civil servants is revealing: It found that out of fifteen different sources of influence, parliamentary committees and MPs were ranked almost at the bottom of the ladder—and that their influence was perceived to be still declining.

Part of the problem is that Parliament does not have the resources to hold the government to account. A complete mismatch now exists between the kinds of resources the executive branch has at its disposal for policy advice compared to that available to Parliament. The Department of Finance alone, with virtually no program responsibility, has far more high-powered policy research capacity and advisors than all of Parliament. Nor is Finance the only central agency in this position. Neither the Privy Council Office nor Treasury Board Secretariat has program responsibilities. Line departments also have substantial policy advice and evaluation capacity. Ministers and their permanent officials have access to a veritable army of consultants, government-funded think tanks, and research groups of one kind or another, all for the most part located in Ottawa.

Consultants and think tanks much prefer dealing with the executive than with Parliament because there is more work to be had in government departments, the work is perceived somehow to be less partisan in nature, and it pays more. They also know better than most that influence —let alone power— lies in the executive, not in Parliament.

In any event, Parliament simply does not have the resources to retain seasoned policy advisors. We therefore need to redirect some policy resources to Parliament, more specifically to opposition parties and to parliamentary committees. I write "redirect" because there is no need to add new positions or to generate new spending.

At the moment, Parliament has about eighty nonpartisan policy researchers. That is about the size of a typical policy shop in a large federal government department although smaller than that available to a central agency. The eighty researchers must serve both houses of Parliament, including parliamentary committees, and respond to specific inquiries from individual members of Parliament.

Clerks of parliamentary committees currently are relatively junior in rank and their role is simply to look after the administrative matters. Things would be vastly different if they were hired at the assistant deputy minister level with a mandate to review broad policy issues and if the staff of the Parliamentary Research Branch grew from 80 to 400, with the extra people drawn from other government policy shops.

But other reforms are needed, starting with the Senate. There is no longer any place in a democracy for an unelected legislative body, a fact that should be obvious even to the most jaded political observer. Australia, a federation with a parliamentary system of government, did something about it some time ago and Canada now needs to follow suit. I prefer an elected, effective, and equal Senate. To those who claim that this is simply not possible, given our past constitutional impasse, I would point out that there is nothing in the Constitution to stop the prime minister from declaring that henceforth he would only appoint senators who had been elected in their own province. If the prime minister would do this, it would revitalize the Senate, very likely reshaping its role in relation both to the prime minister and to the House of Commons.

There are several reasons why the Supreme Court has a growing legitimacy problem. To be sure, the fact that it has had to deal with more controversial issues, given the Charter of Rights and Freedoms, is one. But there are others. The appointment process needs to be completely overhauled. At the moment, the prime minister has the unfettered power to appoint all Supreme Court judges. As with the Senate, the current appointment process to the Supreme Court belongs to the prime minister, not to Canadians. This situation is no longer acceptable. Canadians have every right to ask who are these people making fundamental decisions that have an impact on their lives, where do they come from, and what are their views on important issues?

The appointment process needs to be made much more transparent. Provincial premiers and the Canadian Bar Association should be formally consulted before the prime minister proposes a candidate and the results of this consultation should be made public, not as a *fait accompli*, but as a proposal. The candidate should also be submitted to a Senate committee for approval and the review should be open to the media and the public.

Reforming the Public Service

The national public service also needs to be reformed. Its role is far more important now in the lives of Canadians, in the national economy, and in shaping public policy than at the time Canada was born. For the most part, the senior public service is located in Ottawa. Indeed, apart from three regional development agencies, federal government departments have virtually all their policy, planning, and evaluation capacity located in Ottawa. The organizational capacity to represent regional circumstances in the machinery of government scarcely exists. The assumption is that this function properly belongs to politicians.

With the Senate incapable of taking on the job, it is left to the Commons, the cabinet, and more importantly, to the prime minister, to incorporate regional circumstances in national policy making. Ontario and Quebec have dominated the Commons, cabinet, and the Prime Minister's Office for virtually all of the last century, and there is no reason to believe that things will be much different in this century. The fact that the national capacity is located in the heart of central Canada and that one secures power by winning the largest number of votes in the Commons will ensure that the interests of Ontario and Quebec will continue to dominate the policy-making process.

What about the public service? It is public servants, not politicians, who prepare the first draft of policy proposals. Data on the regional composition of federal public servants such as province of birth and postsecondary education are difficult to secure. However, a survey of the 220 most senior officials carried out several years ago revealed that only 10% were born or educated in western Canada, and 4% in Atlantic Canada.

At the moment, one needs to have a working knowledge of both official languages to become an assistant deputy minister or deputy minister in Ottawa. The federal government could establish a policy that, henceforth, one would also need to have served as a public servant outside of Ontario and Quebec—that is, in the north, western provinces, or Atlantic Canada —before making it to the senior ranks of the federal public service. That would promote a greater understanding of Canada's regions and regional circumstances as policy proposals are in the planning stages.

Canada, at its core, is regional and everything Canadian is regional: politics, culture, language, and economic development. Michael Marzolini, the Liberal government's pollster, made a presentation to the party's biennial convention in Ottawa in March 2000, pointing out, perhaps to the surprise of some delegates, that the "Liberals do well in Ontario because voters there see no difference between the national and provincial interests." He added that things are very different in other regions. Marzolini's polls simply make the case that for those in western and Atlantic Canada, "national" policy is a code word that actually means a regional policy for Ontario.

Canada, at least the outer Canada, no longer harbours any hope that our national, political, judicial, and administrative institutions can serve all of Canada without major surgery. Outer Canadians love Canada, but not the arrangements they live under. We need to reform our national institutions so they are more open, accountable, and sensitive to the country's regional, political, and economic realities.

Sheelagh Whittaker

Sheelagh Whittaker | *until Spring 2001 was president and CEO of EDS Canada Inc., a professional information technology services company, and a corporate vice-president of EDS.* Currently, she serves as managing director of government business with EDS Australia. Before joining EDS, she was president and CEO of Canadian Satellite Communications Inc., and vice-president of planning and corporate affairs for the Canadian Broadcasting Network. She began her career as a combines investigation officer for the Department of Consumer and Corporate Affairs, after obtaining an MBA from York University, a Bachelor of Science degree from University of Alberta, and a Bachelor of Arts degree from University of Toronto.

SHEELAGH WHITTAKER
Past President and CEO,
EDS Canada

33 Yonge Street, Suite 601
Toronto, ON • M5E 1G4

MEMORANDUM

To: **The Prime Minister of Canada**

From: **Sheelagh Whittaker** | *Managing Director,*
Government Business, EDS Australia

Subject: **Leadership in a Digital Age**

I want to share with you my amazement at the magic, the wonder, and the empowerment afforded by the digital economy. Although many cannot yet see the profound change that the digital economy will bring to the lives of each and every Canadian, that's okay—they will see it soon enough. The range of individual freedom and choice offered by the digital economy, the freedom to choose where and how we want to live—and to be able to do it on our own terms—is truly the stuff of revolution!

But new responsibility comes with all new freedoms. And here too, our government faces fresh challenges as it grapples with new forms of governance that are appropriate for the digital economy. A balanced approach will be required that acknowledges issues of privacy, service delivery, and international relationship management. As the information age and the digital economy continue to change and take shape, Canadians will continue to be increasingly affected by (and involved in) the direction our government takes in providing services and information on-line.

The new form of governance required by the new information age must focus on the citizen as its customer and its shareholder. This governance must address new alliances formed in the face of converging technologies. And it must provide reasonable governance for new public and private partnerships.

An emerging model for governance and government operations in the digital economy will fly in the face of standard archetypes. It will be, obviously, digital-based and call on such technologies as the Internet, interactive TV, call centres, mobile communications and kiosks, rather than on the current bureaucratic model of government.

The drivers of this new governance model will be newer imperatives such as citizen expectations, improved responsiveness, more convenience, and more flexible policies. And it will hinge on government re-invention of itself to meet those new performance measures.

As the digital economy continues to extend its reach into our lives, our businesses, and our consciousness, it will also continue to alter the forms of governance we have traditionally known. Overall, it will increase citizen "ownership" of the policy-making and legislative processes.

That will require more flexibility, more responsiveness, and greater creativity on the part of governments as they strive to stay ahead of the curve and provide the leadership, connection, and accessibility that citizens will demand. A government will be measured by its citizens against other governments around the world through the manner in which it accommodates those new realities and through its response to those new demands.

That poses enormous challenges for the Government of Canada. Not only must it provide citizens with a smooth, seamless, technically flawless channel and routing to information and services on demand, it must deliver those services in a hermetically sealed environment that preserves individual privacy and safeguards information security. And as if those challenges were not enough, government leaders face a new reality in which government performance has become a new point of comparison in the relentless global competition for investment and revenue. Technology-driven global integration of markets has accelerated the influence and impact of market forces on national governments. It has certainly affected their economies. In an age where billions of dollars can be moved into and out of countries over the course of an afternoon by dispassionate and distinctly un-nationalistic investors whose main dominion is the click of a button, the reputation, stability, and *performance* of governments become key measurements to success.

I applaud our federal government for its determination to become a leader in presenting the world with an organized, relevant, on-line presence that will portray Canada as an attractive country in which to live, visit, and do business. But even though there's no question that the government has the very best of "product" to work with, it still, nonetheless, has its work cut out for it.

As with most other governments swept into the slipstream of new technologies, Canada's federal government must contend with several serious issues if it hopes to establish and maintain the *orderly* growth of access to and service from on-line sources. In an environment of fiscal restraint and prudent resource management, it cannot afford to discard or rewrite existing systems. Never has the catch phrase "doing more with less" been so strident or so challenging.

The government can no longer afford the luxury of that wonderful cushion called "the fullness of time" in which to ponder and ruminate. It needs systems in place and up and running—*now!*

Privacy and Security: Today's Peace, Order, and Good Government

Through its obligations to provide an environment of regulatory peace, order, and good government, it has to pay very close attention to the issues of privacy and security I have mentioned. Legislation such as Bill C-6, the privacy bill, may face those issues head-on for today but it may all have to be rewritten tomorrow.

In providing all of the bedrock e-government services online—services such as the payment of taxes, the renewal of licences, or the registration of property—our governments have to look for ways of adding value to the process. They have to actively pursue new alliances and public-private partnerships that will enhance levels of compliance and delivery. They have to provide *thought* leadership as well as legislative leadership. They have to help shape business processes that walk the fine line between entrepreneurial free-for-alls and incentive-squashing over-regulation. And they have to pay attention to relationship management as they reach out to the private sector and other government organizations at every level.

Such relationships can only be founded on trust. In fact, trust was cited as the key element for digital economy success by more than 80% of respondents in an EDS-commissioned poll in September 2000. In that survey, 87% of respondents said unauthorized sharing of personal information was the area of most concern.

Why that concern? Well, to start, reports of cyber crime-related incidents are becoming far too common. From hackers to breaches of government systems to insidious e-mail viruses that paralyze systems around the world.

We cannot afford to have the digital economy and the Internet remain as vulnerable as they are today. There is no single solution to cyber security. And everyone has a role to play. For starters, "cyber ethics" must become a regular and understandable part of the Internet lexicon. We have to begin teaching our young people that hacking is not cool.

Internet security is also crucial to building an enduring culture of Internet commerce in Canada and around the world. Canadians have clearly embraced the Internet but many remain wary of buying on-line. A recent national survey conducted by Ipsos-Reid (formerly Angus Reid) shows that 73% of Internet users in Canada have never made a purchase on-line. Of those, 74% say their hesitancy in buying on-line is based on fears about the security of giving their credit card information over the Internet.

From a more global perspective, industry and government are cooperating fully to search for effective and fair resolutions. Although nobody has all the answers, only by working together will we identify and act on the complex issues that require attention on an international scale.

What Government and Industry Must Do

There are a number of actions I believe industry must take. Initially, cooperate with governments, especially law-enforcement authorities where appropriate. Under transparent conditions, execute those actions while continuing to protect individual privacy according to national law. Second, take the lead. As primary owners and operators of the Internet, industry has primary responsibility for security. Third, share information about threats and vulnerabilities, company to company, and cooperate with governments in reporting attacks and incidents of cyber crime. Lastly, inform governments about barriers or deterrents to sharing information. Existing laws, for example, do not address liability concerns.

Concurrently, government can also play an instrumental role in creating the right conditions and the right environment to allow the digital economy to offer the security that Canadians have come to expect in day-to-day commerce. Those actions include the following:

- Involve industry in achieving international agreements to fight cyber crime. Regional agreements lack the enforcement reach to address the global nature of cyber crime.
- Clarify criminal laws to make them clear and interoperable for all forms of cyber crimes and ensure those laws are enforced.
- Strive not to increase the regulatory burden. That threatens our chance of success.
- Ensure on-line conduct is judged in a legal manner consistent with off-line conduct.
- Avoid shifting the government costs of cyber crime fighting directly to industry players doing business on the Internet.
- Cooperate government to government so law enforcement investigative processes permitted in one country do not violate another country's laws.

At the same time, business users of the Internet must build security into their Internet business models, instead of treating security as an "add-on" feature. Without security, users will not build the trust so necessary to the digital economy. The goal: to ensure the global Internet is safe, reliable, and always accessible.

The digital economy is erasing national borders, removing economic barriers, and enabling companies to become truly global. The digital economy links business with customers and suppliers in ways never dreamed of five years ago when the term World Wide Web first took hold. But this digital economy of ours is just in its infancy—and its future depends on trust and security. Together, companies and governments must step up to address this global challenge. Not taking action is not an option. Business and governments must invest in cyber security. If not, the digital economy of the twenty-first century—and Canada's opportunity to reap its benefits—may flounder.

David Conklin
Mary Crossan

David Conklin | *holds the James D. Fleck Chair in International Business at the Richard Ivey School of Business at the University of Western Ontario.* He teaches in the Global Environment of Business group, which focuses on the ways in which the economic, political, societal, and technological forces differ among countries throughout the world, and which analyzes business strategies in the context of these forces. Prior to joining the business school, he was employed in research institutes, the Ontario government, small business corporations, and several government task forces and royal commissions. He earned a B.A. in political science and economics from the University of Toronto and a Ph.D. in economics from the Massachusetts Institute of Technology.

Mary Crossan | *holds the Donald K. Jackson Chair in Entrepreneurship and is an associate professor of strategic management at the Richard Ivey School of Business at the University of Western Ontario.* Her research on organizational learning, strategy, and improvisation has been widely published in journals and she has extended her research to management practice through a collection of over thirty cases, many of which have been published in a book she co-authored, *Strategic Management: A Canadian Casebook.* In a joint venture between the business school and the Second City Improvisation Company, she developed a management video entitled "Improvise to Innovate," which extends traditional concepts of strategic management to develop tools and techniques for more innovative, flexible, and responsive strategic action.

Richard Ivey School of Business

The University of Western Ontario

1151 Richmond Street North
London, Ontario, Canada N6A 3K7

E-mail: info@ivey.uwo.ca
Internet: http://www.ivey.uwo.ca

Tel: (519) 661 3206
Fax: (519) 661 3485

MEMORANDUM

To: The Prime Minister of Canada

From: David Conklin and Mary Crossan | *Professors, Richard Ivey School of Business*

Subject: **Public Sector Management in the Twenty-First Century: Lessons from the Private Sector**

The political, economic, social, and technological environments are changing quickly and in significant ways for corporations and governments. In business, those changes have led to new paradigms for corporate decision-making and management. Many concepts and routines that were widely accepted a decade ago are being replaced with new perspectives and new practices. Those managerial approaches by businesses could provide guidance in rethinking government. In this memo, we identify five promising areas.

1. Vision

As the pace of change has increased, so too has the importance of vision as a means to anchor the corporation. The vision provides a broad strategic direction and also creates a "corporate culture" that serves as an integrating force, providing implicit encouragement and emotional support for everyone in the common dedication to the achievement of the vision.

In recent years the economic imperative to get Canada's financial house in order has dominated the government agenda. However, the time has come for a bolder vision for Canada. While there are many possibilities, the vision we advocate is one centring on human capital. This is consistent with the four remaining areas for action we identify, and was also advocated by Queen's professor Tom Courchene, an academic whom you know well. He published a book in 2000 suggesting that the vision of human capital should form the basis for the re-evaluation and restructuring of all your government policies.

2. An E-Government Mission

In view of the meltdown in dot-com corporations you may be tempted to dismiss the potentially enormous opportunities that the Internet is creating for your government. While the enhancement of human capital should be your vision for the nation, the careful application of new information technologies could form an important element of your government's mission.

The increasing use of computers and information systems has "flattened" business organizations, reducing the number of people in middle management. Information systems have long been present in the workplace but until recently they were unable to interface with other information systems within the organization. The introduction of integrated business application software in the past decade has changed that situation by standardizing information systems, integrating data in real time from all business functions, and linking the company's business processes and applications. We recommend a similar ongoing evaluation and restructuring of government procedures and services in response to these new technologies, just as has been occurring in business. In fact, we recommend that you adapt the perspective of "e-government," the mirror image of "e-business."

The implementation of sophisticated integrated information systems has opened up a wealth of organizational design possibilities for businesses in Canada. Depending on each firm's particular situation, strategy, differentiation, and imagination, many more functions may be affected by this technology in the future. Virtual workplaces and telework are increasingly popular models for connecting workers and managers, leading to improvements in productivity, profits, and customer service. We suggest that your government, like a corporate head office, may benefit from an analysis of how new technologies could encourage structures and practices that are more effective and that enhance innovation and quality improvements.

3. The Decomposition of Organizational Boundaries

In the past, the size of a corporation was largely determined by the transaction costs and transportation costs that would arise if activities were conducted in separate firms. What was cheaper to accomplish internally got done internally. The telecommunications revolution has reduced transaction costs among corporations and has facilitated the inter-corporate flow of information.

In the twenty-first century, the connection a firm will have with its suppliers, their suppliers, and its customers is more like an interconnected web, rather than a sequential chain. A chain implies a unidirectional exchange along a distinct flow, whereas a web suggests interconnectedness and multidirectional, multilevel relationships that can lead to better and faster innovations. Innovation today requires that all parties interact on an ongoing, extended basis. If the initial producer of the components knows the needs of the ultimate user of its products, it can better design for that purpose. If there is a free exchange of information and communication, all parties benefit from decreased development times, assured market acceptance, and continual, planned future offerings.

How can your government more effectively participate in, and stimulate the success of, such creative webs with businesses and citizens? As an example of what you can do, we point to your support for business-university government research centres. We recommend the extension of this concept to other activities, such as health care delivery, retraining, and the provision of welfare. In the future, we encourage you to rethink the provision of all government services and funding to achieve the collaboration of business and citizens in more direct ways.

Globalization adds a complication to innovation and this creative web. With current communications and transportation technology, outsourcing can involve any country in the world, and as such, each corporation has a wide selection of alternative potential suppliers. Here, the creative web becomes a geographical web. Coordinating this complex network so that it involves an ongoing innovation process has become a key determinant of company success. In what ways and to what degree can Canadian government activities be linked with activities in other countries? Can globalization offer opportunities to your government as it has to businesses?

As the twentieth century drew to a close, academics began to discuss various aspects of the decomposition and decentralization of the corporation. A crucial element will be hierarchy and cooperation. We suggest that as the twenty-first century advances, corporations will be shifting from a low level of cooperation and a high degree of hierarchy to a high level of cooperation and a low degree of hierarchy. We suggest that your government as well should be shifting in that direction.

This decomposition of organizational boundaries and the creation of new structures are linked clearly with the concept of mirroring e-business in e-government. In their book *Blueprint to the Digital Economy: Creating Wealth in the Era of E-Business*, Don Tapscott, Alex Lowy, and David Ticoll look at corporations that have changed their structure in response to new communication technologies. Business sectors where such transformations have been common include banking, publishing, and education. No doubt government will also benefit from the possibilities.

In today's increasingly dynamic business environment, business leaders have been forced into focusing their organization's attention on the strategic, value-added components of their organization. Activities deemed nonessential are increasingly being outsourced to experienced service providers. This new competitive reality has led to the formation of strategic alliances between organizations that focus on product and service development and those that focus on client service and integration. We recommend this literature and those corporate experiences as you examine how to improve the effectiveness of government.

4. Enhancing International Competitiveness

Harvard professor Michael Porter in his influential work on competitiveness has emphasized that no nation has a competitive advantage with regard to all economic activities. He identified four elements that make a nation competitive in certain types of industries:

a. Factor conditions: The nation's position in factors of production—such as skilled labour or infrastructure—necessary to compete in a given industry. Porter emphasizes that the value of particular factors can be dramatically altered by the choice of technology, and most factors must be developed over time through investment.

He distinguishes between generalized factors such as the educational level of the labour force or the highway system and specialized factors such as personnel with specific skills or infrastructure geared to specific industries. Competitive advantage based on basic or generalized factors is unsophisticated and often fleeting. Specialized factors provide a more decisive and sustainable basis for competitive advantage. They require more focus and often riskier private and social investment. Leadership is required to define a vision for investment in specialized factors.

b. *Demand conditions: The nature of home demand for the industry's product or service.* The competitiveness of an industry rests on ready access to a large group of purchasers of its products. The size of a nation's market for a certain product may determine the economies of scale or the degree of knowledge and skill in a particular industry. A large number of independent buyers may stimulate innovation since each has its own ideas about product needs. As well, an early saturation of domestic demand may create incentives to modify products, cut costs, and reduce prices, and these reactions can make an industry more competitive internationally. Given these "demand" factors, the terms and conditions in the trade agreements that you negotiate are particularly important.

c. *Related and supporting industries: The presence or absence in the nation of supplier industries and related industries that are internationally competitive.* The competitiveness of an industry will depend on its ability to purchase cost-effective inputs. Consequently, a particular industry's competitiveness depends on the strength of its domestic suppliers. The industry may work with its suppliers to create input modifications that can support its competitiveness. From this perspective as well, a particular industry's competitiveness depends on the competitiveness of its suppliers, and here again the degree to which your trade agreements integrate our businesses with those of other nations will play a key role in our international competitiveness.

d. Firm strategy, structure, and rivalry: The conditions in the nation governing how companies are created, organized, and managed, and the nature of domestic rivalry. Competitiveness also depends upon an industry's organizational structure. Management practices unique to a certain nation may give particular industries a competitiveness advantage. Within a nation, the greater the intensity of competition, the greater the likelihood of innovation of various kinds. Consequently, an important foundation for future international competitiveness is the domestic rivalry within particular industries. Here the role and practices of Canada's Competition Bureau are crucial. It will be important to re-evaluate the bureau in the context of the significant changes in technologies that seem to be accelerating both international and national mergers and acquisitions.

Your government has a key role to play in enhancing the competitiveness of Canadian business in each of those four categories that Porter highlights.

5. *Leveraging Intellectual Capital Through Organizational Learning*

Many businesses are recognizing that the only sustainable competitive advantage is their ability to learn more quickly than their competitors. Since the most valuable resource of the business walks out of the building at the end of the day, firms must leverage their intellectual capital through organizational learning. Many firms have come to recognize that they have high stocks of intellectual capital vested in individuals, teams, and learning that have become institutionalized in the organization. The primary challenge is to unlock the bottlenecks in the flow of learning from individuals and groups to the organization (which can be called feed-forward), and from the organization back to individuals and groups (the more traditional feedback). Often learning that has become institutionalized creates unwanted bureaucracy that can hinder the feedback flow that prompts learning itself. Worse yet, it stifles innovation and insight, which need to arise through the feed-forward flow of learning. Frustration arises, motivation declines, and ultimately the best employees leave the organization (or the country). Our research shows that one of the biggest barriers to effective organizational learning is the leadership itself.

The implications for government are two-fold. First, to enhance organizational learning within the government, leadership development requires placing at the top of the agenda what it takes to lead—not just to manage—a government department. Central to leadership is managing the organizational learning infrastructure to achieve the identified strategic objectives. In particular, since bureaucracy can ossify the system, leadership needs to continually prune bureaucracy to ensure that the institutionalized learning continues to support the needs of the government department and the Canadian citizens it serves.

The second implication for government is to understand its role within the organizational learning system of the larger economy. Just as leadership within an organization can create a barrier to organizational learning, so too government can stifle the capacity of the country to learn. In the same way that management cannot ignore concerns by employees that their voice is not being heard or that the organization does not provide the systems, technology, data, or processes to do their job, so too must government take a leadership role in listening to business and providing a more optimal learning infrastructure. The challenge here is significant since it is not only leadership in the government that needs to adopt this thinking. It must, in fact, run through to the front lines of government.

Conclusion

We are hopeful that our message is consistent and clear: Canada needs a bold vision, which provides investment in and leverages human capital. Through technology and a more effective organizational learning infrastructure, Canada will continually adapt to the rapid change in the global environment. The government and your leadership are instrumental in making this happen.

ECONOMIC
CANADA

A. Charles Baillie

Catherine Swift

David Pecaut

John Loxley

*Jason Clemens and
Joel Emes*

Bruce O'Hara

Part Two

A. Charles Baillie

A. Charles Baillie *is chairman and CEO of the TD Bank Financial Group.* Under his leadership it has become arguably the most dynamic Canadian bank, with an increasingly strong presence both domestically and globally. Mr. Baillie began his career at TD in 1964, progressing through a number of positions. As vice-president and general manager, he launched TD's U.S. division, and as executive vice-president, corporate and investment-banking group, he was responsible for building TD Securities. He was appointed chief executive officer in 1997 and added the role of chairman in early 1998. Mr. Baillie grew up in Orillia, Ontario, and graduated from the University of Toronto's Trinity College in 1962 with an Honours Bachelor of Arts Degree in Political Science and Economics. He earned his M.B.A. from Harvard Business School in 1964. Mr. Baillie is a director of several corporations and is involved in numerous charitable and artistic organizations, including serving as chairman of the United Way Campaign in 2000. He is also a director of Calmeadow, a non-profit organization specializing in microfinance. He has spoken out passionately in favour of national unity, in addition to health care.

ECONOMIC
CANADA

A. Charles Baillie
Chairman
and Chief Executive Officer

MEMORANDUM

To: **The Prime Minister of Canada**

From: A. **Charles Baillie** | *Chairman and CEO,*
TD Bank Financial Group

Subject: **Resuming Our Place as a Leader on the World
Stage: Setting an Ambitious Goal for Canada**

I would like to suggest an ambitious goal for Canada—one that
would see us fundamentally rethink our future and outpace the
United States in growth within fifteen years.

One of the key tests of our nation's health is how the economy is performing, and this is where I would like to see us
focusing more of our energy and efforts.

The question on everyone's mind as I write has been: How
will the recent U.S. slowdown affect Canada? Will there be a
recession? How deep might any downturn be? And how long
will it be before the economy recovers?

The damage done by the recessions of the early 1980s and
1990s set Canada's economic and social progress back, not just
for the periods that were officially defined as recession, but
also for many subsequent years. The ugly result is that for the
last decade and a half our living standard has declined relative
to that in the United States. And, even more discouraging, it
has also declined relative to an increasing number of other
countries—countries that have traditionally trailed us, such as
Denmark and Norway.

Real disposable income per person—that is, what remains after we pay income tax and contribute to the Canada Pension Plan and Employment Insurance—began and ended the decade at precisely the same level. By this comprehensive measure, over the last decade of the century, Canadians saw absolutely no improvement in their standard of living.

One might logically conclude that we maintained the status quo. But the trap of statistics, and particularly averages, is that they can hide unpleasant truths. The fact is that the income distribution gap widened during the 1990s. What is particularly discouraging is that the standard of living for many of our lower-income groups actually dropped.

And while we've had our eye on the U.S. economy ahead of us in the left lane, we've paid little attention to the fact that a number of other economies have zoomed by us in the right lane. In 1990, Canada had the fourth highest standard of living within the OECD economies. By 1999, we had sunk to seventh as Japan, Norway, and Denmark overtook us. In the last 15 years, while our real income per capita plummeted from 86% to 78% of the U.S. standard of living, Ireland soared from 47% to 76%. A country that was among the poorest in Europe 15 years ago now almost matches our living standard. In fact, looking at the twenty-eight countries the International Monetary Fund classifies as "advanced," Canada had the fourth worst cumulative growth rate over the past fifteen years.

Those statistics are troubling, and I relay them here not to cast aspersions but to set a context for the plan I would like to see us adopt as a country. That plan would set a goal that would return Canada to what I believe is its reasonable place as a growth leader in the world economy. It will help us achieve our social objectives by strengthening the fundamentals of our economy, making us more competitive commercially as well as financially, and increasing the economic pie for all Canadians to share. It will give us the resources to tackle and resolve our social issues without putting future generations into hock.

I am suggesting that our goal should be to increase our standard of living so that in fifteen years it is not just equal to the United States, but it is better.

Now, let me acknowledge that this is a very ambitious goal. Can the mouse outrun the elephant? If Luxembourg, with a very much smaller population than ours, can do it, I have no doubt that we have the capacity to do so. I believe that if we set our minds to it, if we work in unison, if we put some passion behind it, we absolutely can challenge the elephant's growth.

But what do we have to do to achieve that goal?

On average, we have to have 1.6-percentage points faster growth than the United States, every year, for 15 years. That will be challenging, certainly, but we have some very solid strengths that bode well for the future.

Our first strength, a decade of low inflation, has kept a lid on borrowing costs for households and corporations. And it is giving the Bank of Canada the flexibility to address potential economic weakness by lowering interest rates. In addition, to their credit, governments at both the federal and provincial levels have turned chronic deficits into surpluses.

Our second strength is that most jurisdictions have started tax relief plans that are lowering personal and corporate income taxes. That relief will sharpen the incentives to Canadians to work, save, and invest, and put Canada in a much more favourable competitive position vis-à-vis the United States and other economies.

Our third strength is that our economy has been diversifying successfully into the so-called new economy industries. Over the past four years, the new economy has contributed between one-quarter and one-third of Canada's overall economic growth each year. The technology that inspired the "new economy" has spread throughout the entire economy; as it reaches into more traditional sectors, industries such as mining and logging become leading edge in their use of technology.

Our fourth strength is that Canada has begun to enjoy the benefits of globalization. Canadian industry used to be a target for foreign takeovers. Today there is more Canadian acquisition of foreign companies than foreign acquisition of Canadian companies. In 1999 Canadian direct investment abroad was more than $257 billion compared with foreign direct investment in Canada of $240 billion.

By expanding markets globally, our domestic companies can benefit from economies of scale that lead to more profits for reinvestment, more cost-effective investment in technology, more jobs, and more income and taxes generated in Canada.

That's the positive side of the ledger. We have already taken many of the steps required to exceed the United States' standard of living, but there is much left to do. The plan I suggest involves four economic levers: debt, taxes, education, and globalization.

At its peak, the federal debt-to-GDP ratio was 71% in fiscal 1996. As of March 2000, it had dropped to just below 59%. That's a significant achievement—but let's look at the broader picture. All we have done is rewind the clock to where we were in the late 1980s.

For every tax dollar we submit this year, 24 cents will go to pay interest on our debt. That money is paying for past consumption. It is not available to invest in strategies to achieve accelerated growth. To spur growth, the debt burden simply must continue to come down, and at a faster pace.

I don't believe that has to happen at the expense of providing some form of personal tax relief. At the same time, it would be naïve to think that lowering the Canadian tax burden would cure all that ails our economy. Again, to their credit, our federal and provincial governments have been cutting personal income taxes recently. But in a few years, when the promised cuts have been fully implemented, Canada's personal income tax burden will still be the highest in the G-7 group of western countries.

Much could be gained by going further and creating a distinctive advantage in the tax area. As Ireland discovered, this led to the creation of large sectors in their domestic economy—sectors that barely existed before. Electronics manufacturing, software development, and financial institutions are examples. Why not make it more attractive to locate in Canada than in the United States?

Complaining about personal and corporate taxes has almost become a cottage industry, but we often overlook the treatment of capital in Canada. Capital is a primary engine of growth in today's technology-charged economies. It certainly has been the force behind the tremendous U.S. expansion in productivity and output in recent years.

In all but one Canadian province, corporations pay capital taxes that are almost four times the burden companies face in the United States. If we are serious about supporting growth in output, jobs, and income, we have to eliminate capital taxes.

While I do advocate lower personal and capital taxes, I am not in the camp of those who would decimate government spending. The debate that says government spending is either all good or all bad is too simplistic. I believe that there are areas where governments should be allocating funds—education and public infrastructure are examples.

At precisely the time when the "knowledge-based" economy is crying out for better educated workers—people who can think and solve problems—we have seen a shocking decline in education spending. In the United States, government spending on public universities in the last two decades increased 20% per student. In Canada spending decreased 30%.

The best and the brightest people in our country are our intellectual pioneers—they make discoveries, develop theories, create new companies, and strengthen existing companies. Those initiatives generate jobs and taxable income for a broad array of people and, in turn, strengthen the safety net for all Canadians.

Our universities don't just incubate new academic theories; they fuel research that leads to the development of industrial clusters around the campus. Those clusters in turn feed new knowledge, new questions, and new experience back into the universities. It is no coincidence that the United States is the world leader in patents.

We are beginning to tackle the huge imbalance between investment in the Canadian and American education systems. Three years ago, your government created the Canada Foundation for Innovation, to invest public money in infrastructure in universities, colleges, and research hospitals. I would also commend the federal government on its creation of 2,000 new research chairs at Canadian universities in 2000, as well as the launch of 13 new institutes of health.

We are on the right track, but we need to do more. Education is not just good economic policy. It is also the best social policy. However, if Canada is to achieve the increased standard of living I have proposed, we have to take even more aggressive action, and very soon.

To reach our standard of living goal we will have to spend heavily on people, not just new academic offices, classrooms, and lecture halls. Investment in post-secondary education pays back a significant return in the vital research and development capabilities that universities attract around them.

For a developed nation, Canada has a dismal performance on the research and development front. We are only 15 among OECD countries in expenditure on research and development. The finance minister has set a target of being among the top five. He has committed to doubling federal expenditures on R&D.

But the private sector, including my own industry and company, needs to be part of the solution as well. We too need to foster more innovation to fuel the growth we need to meet our standard of living objective.

We need to acknowledge also that we limit ourselves if we have our sights set only on domestic markets. To be successful and significant international players, companies have to achieve a certain scale. In many private sector groups, including banking, we as a country have not yet come to terms with how best to take advantage of business opportunities in markets outside the country. That is one area where the private and public sectors could work together.

I began by suggesting a goal of overtaking the U.S. standard of living within 15 years. To meet that goal, we will have to boldly change what we do and how we do it. Government, academia, labour, and business will have to work closely together to agree upon goals, and the means of achieving those goals.

I have suggested that continuing to drive our debt down, lowering taxes, investing intelligently in education, and turning our sights to the opportunities that globalization affords us will increase our chance of resuming our place as a leader on the world stage. We can accomplish that only if our various constituencies agree upon the goal and work together to achieve it.

Robertson Davies wrote that "Canada is not a country you love, it's a country you worry about." Personally, I believe there is a lot to love about Canada and I think it's time we stopped worrying and started acting.

Catherine Swift

Catherine Swift *is president, CEO, and chairwoman of the Canadian Federation of Independent Business,* an organization she has served in a variety of senior capacities since joining it in 1987 as vice-president of research and chief economist. Ms. Swift worked with the federal government in Ottawa from 1976 to 1983, holding several positions with the departments of Consumer and Corporate Affairs, Industry, and Communications. Her areas of specialization included corporate and industrial analysis, international trade, and computer communications. From 1983 to 1987, she was senior economist with the Toronto-Dominion Bank. Ms. Swift studied at the University of Toronto and Carleton University in Ottawa, obtaining a B.A. (Honours) in Economics in 1977 and an M.A. in Economics in 1980. She is a member of the board of directors of The Empire Club and a director of the C.D. Howe Institute.

ECONOMIC
CANADA

CANADIAN FEDERATION OF
INDEPENDENT BUSINESS

4141 Yonge St., Suite 401
Willowdale, ON M2P 2A6
Telephone: (416) 222-8022

MEMORANDUM

To: **The Prime Minister of Canada**

From: **Catherine Swift** | *President and CEO,*
Canadian Federation of Independent Business

Subject: **A "Do-It-Yourself" Society**

There's an old saying that if you want to own a small business in Canada, you should buy a big business and wait a while. Although the sentiment conveyed by this is firmly tongue in cheek, it does provide some truth in suggesting the element of challenge involved in operating a successful small business in Canada. Fortunately, the reality over the past few decades is that a growing number of Canadians are rising to the challenge and achieving success in the small business sphere.

If you scratch the surface of Canada's entrepreneurial explosion in recent years, you will find that in addition to the predictable business elements there is a set of values that underlie the entrepreneurial motivation. Those values do not have to be limited to the business sphere. Indeed, I believe that a greater focus in Canada on promoting and extending these values and qualities to all elements of Canadian society would position our nation very well for the challenges facing us in the coming years.

Although it is impossible to fit entrepreneurs neatly into any one category, research has consistently identified a number of common entrepreneurial qualities. Those common elements include such things as the desire to be one's own boss, independence, self-reliance, the desire to build something, and the need to make a contribution to society. There is also a powerful anti-establishment undercurrent to the entrepreneurial mindset, accompanied by a fundamental skepticism of big bureaucracies such as those found in government and large corporations. Although money is certainly one motivating factor, it has never been found to be the leading incentive for entrepreneurs. Most entrepreneurs have experienced spectacular failure as well as fantastic success; in fact, surviving the former is often a prerequisite for achieving the latter.

One of the strengths of Canada's entrepreneurial culture is that we have allowed people to fail. To see what happens in societies that do not believe in letting businesses fail, we need only to look at the serious problems currently plaguing many countries around the world, where governments had propped up inefficient and sometimes corrupt companies and financial institutions as long as possible, until finally the whole house of cards came crashing down. The Asian economies, for example, are now in for many years of economic instability before they can be normalized again. Ironically, several years ago some Canadian observers singled out Japan and their highly interventionist way of managing their economy as a model to be emulated. Not surprisingly, we don't hear too many of those comments today. The way in which Japan and other centrally managed economies conducted their affairs was antithetical to the true nature of entrepreneurship and has ultimately been proven to be a dismal failure.

Negative motivations have also pushed some people into entrepreneurship. Many people have become entrepreneurs because the classic societal power groups—big government, big corporations, and big unions—have excluded them. That has certainly been the case over the past few decades for many immigrants to Canada. Also, over the last twenty years or so, there has been an incredible growth in the number of women entering the ranks of entrepreneurship, in part because they faced resistance in many occupations or encountered the infamous "glass ceiling" in the public or corporate sectors. Many young people also find that in the absence of more traditional employment opportunities the best way to beat the conundrum they faced of "no experience, no job—no job, no experience" is to launch their own enterprises.

International research also illustrates that a society founded on entrepreneurial values enjoys positive spin-offs in many areas other than just business and the economy. The mainstay of most communities is not large corporations but the smaller enterprises that are closely integrated into community activities of all kinds. Most young people find their first job in a small firm. As well, entrepreneurship is the original equal opportunity employer, as no group or individual is excluded. Finally, a vibrant entrepreneurial sector is also essential to a well-functioning democracy. A focus on entrepreneurship can therefore be seen not only as a base for a healthy economy but also as a foundation for a healthy society.

Building On Our Entrepreneurial Heritage

Fortunately, Canada has a healthy entrepreneurial history on which to build. Although we Canadians may have a reputation for being rather subdued and polite, this does not seem to hamper us when it comes to starting and operating businesses. A recent international study of entrepreneurial attitudes in several developed countries found that Canadians were neck-and-neck with Americans as the most entrepreneurial of the bunch. And among the countries surveyed, Canadians were actually the most receptive to the idea that their children should aspire to entrepreneurship—even more so than Americans.

Successive public opinion polls have also shown that the most respected and trusted group in society is small business—far ahead of politicians, large corporations, and labour unions. So it would seem to make sense that a public policy thrust based on entrepreneurial principles and values would be well received by the voting public, and therefore should be an attractive political platform as well.

Canada, in fact, made some progress toward becoming a more entrepreneurial nation throughout the 1990s, as evidenced by the support by a broad range of Canadians for such objectives as getting rid of government deficits and paying down debt—goals that had been advocated by the small business community for years, while many others thought such things as deficits to be relatively unimportant. Canadians have rightly become suspicious of governments that promise to "do it all" for us, now that decades of overspending and overtaxing have left so little to show for it all but enormous debts, and industries and regions whose economies are dependent not on themselves but on the willingness of other regions or sectors to support them. Such support via various forms of transfer payments and high levels of taxation has been one reason why average Canadians have had no increase in their real standard of living for over a decade.

There are some hopeful signs that we are changing direction in a positive way but we still have a very long way to go. For decades, we in Canada have permitted many of our governments to foster a culture of dependence. This process was undertaken with the best of intentions but unfortunately has gone much too far and will now take some time to reverse. After years of dependence on one form of social assistance or another, many Canadians have forgotten how to work, or have, for various reasons, been out of the labour force for so long that they have become unemployable. In the early years of the twenty-first century, we find ourselves with unacceptably high unemployment despite several years of strong economic growth. And this high unemployment coexists with increasingly acute labour shortages in all areas, from entry-level workers up to the very highly skilled. Small- and medium-sized businesses, still the most dominant and dependable job creators in the economy, are finding it increasingly difficult to hire people. This is despite unemployment rates of around 7%—rates that used to be considered disgracefully high, but that now seem to be accepted with resignation as the lowest we can go.

Structural unemployment—that group of the unemployed who are not merely between jobs for a brief period but who are out of the labour force for longer stretches because their skills are outdated or their reliance on social programs has reduced their employability—has grown in Canada throughout each business cycle since the 1970s. Not coincidentally, it was during the 1970s that the welfare state really got rolling in Canada. Throughout the same period, finding people willing and able to work has become more difficult. This growing incidence of structural unemployment is not unique to our country, now that fast-paced technological change has shortened the shelf life of many skills, but it is a serious problem, especially when we compare ourselves to our most important economic partner south of the border.

The Loonie and the Frog

At the same time as unemployment rates have been increasing, we have seen a steady depreciation in the value of the Canadian dollar. It is almost unbelievable to think that the Canadian dollar was at par with the U.S. dollar in 1975, when today too many people have taken for granted seeing it hovering at under two-thirds of the American dollar. The lower value of our dollar may be attractive in the short term to exporters and the tourism industry but a steady devaluation of our currency really represents the gradual impoverishment of our nation and a decline in our standard of living. Maintaining a strong, unique culture is directly linked to a strong economy, and when one suffers, so does the other. All our regional stresses and strains become far more troublesome as our economy and standard of living are dragged down inch by inch by a limp loonie. It is akin to the old story wherein if you throw a frog into boiling water it immediately jumps out but if you put a frog in cold water and gradually heat it the frog doesn't notice the incremental change until it is too late.

Unlike the frog, it is not yet too late for us as Canadians, but we clearly need a change in direction—and soon. The temperature of the water is indeed warming up. In order to take the heat off, it is necessary for Canadians as a whole to embrace the power and vast potential of entrepreneurship. An emphasis on a more entrepreneurial mindset as a nation is a prerequisite for success. Canada has already taken some steps in the right direction, but we must continue on this path and not revert to bad old habits. Our fiscal position as a nation is currently better than it has been in some time. But we must stick to a prudent approach, devoting the lion's share of future surpluses to debt repayment and broadly based income and sales tax reductions, and only very selectively to further spending growth. This would not only stimulate the economy but also permit more latitude for Canadians to make their own choices in areas such as retirement planning and promote a more self-reliant approach to economic issues in general. Recent changes to loosen the Employment Insurance regime were very disappointing, not because they increased the costs of the program dramatically but because they seemed to be sending the message that it was okay to rely on such programs on a regular basis instead of working toward long-term employment. Governments cannot continue to preach how we need to ready ourselves for the new, technologically driven and highly competitive economy of the future while implementing policies that hamper our ability to do so.

Canadians should also put more focus on celebrating and rewarding our entrepreneurial successes. Entrepreneurship should be taught in our public school system at an early stage and be presented as a positive career option, not as a last resort if all else fails. Other complementary measures could include such things as a more widespread offering of cooperative education, policies to encourage employee investments in small- and medium-sized ventures, and amendments to our tax and regulatory regime that currently penalize small, entrepreneurial businesses. Those are just some of the many possible and affordable measures that could be put in place to promote the evolution of Canada as a more entrepreneurial nation and make this country the world leader it has always had the potential to be.

David Pecaut

David Pecaut | *is president of iFormation Group,* where he creates new business models for the Internet space, bringing together prospective partners to build these new ventures and taking equity positions with the objective of creating sustainable value. Prior to joining iFormation, he was the founder and leader of the Boston Consulting Group's global electronic commerce practice and leader of its Canadian practice. Mr. Pecaut's advice has been sought frequently on issues of public policy in North America, South America, Europe, and Asia, and he has served as co-chair of the Canadian E-Business Opportunities Roundtable, a joint private and public sector advisory group on e-commerce. He holds a Master's degree in philosophy from the University of Sussex and an AB magna cum laude from Harvard College.

i Formation

iFormation Group
875 Third Avenue, 5th Floor
New York, NY 10022
T 212 548 6300
F 212 548 6399
www.iformationgroup.com

MEMORANDUM

To: The Prime Minister of Canada

From: David Pecaut | *President,*
iFormation Group

Subject: **The Internet Economy: The Second Inning
of a Nine-Inning Game**

Everything we will hear about the impact of the Internet Revolution over the next three years will probably be over-hyped. But at the same time everything that will happen in the next ten years is almost certainly underestimated.

This remarkable phenomenon is taking shape as a result of three fairly predictable technological drivers. The first driver is Moore's Law, which predicts the doubling of computer power every 18 months. The second is falling telecommunications costs, and the third, often called Metcalfe's Law, says that any new person who joins an existing network of people, such as the World Wide Web, increases the value to everyone else on the network by an exponential number, in fact the square of those already on the network.

It is not difficult to grasp the intellectual underpinnings of these latest advances in technology and understand what's driving the change. The difficulty is fully appreciating what this revolution means for our daily and business lives as Canadians. As prime minister, you can ensure that Canadians keep their sights squarely on the future because in reality we are only in the second inning of a nine-inning game that may well go into extra innings.

The Canadian E-Business Opportunities Roundtable took an in-depth look at Canada's position in the e-business economy two years ago and tracked its progress over the last year. The prognosis: Canada received a passing grade, but achieved uneven performance.

On the positive side, our share of global e-commerce revenues was 5.9% in 1998 and 5.8% in 1999. Not only have we held our own in the growing e-commerce market, but also we have captured a disproportionate share, given the size of the Canadian economy. Over the same period, the U.S. share of global e-commerce shrank from 74.3% to 61.3%, losing ground as other countries improved their own e-business competitiveness.

However, our ability to maintain our global share of the Internet economy is by no means assured. Global competition is escalating. According to IDC, a leading provider of technology intelligence, Canada's share of global e-commerce will shrink to 3.9% of a $4-trillion market by 2004. We will need to work hard to maintain Canada's target of 5% of global e-commerce trade.

That will be important for a number of reasons—most critically job creation throughout the economy. E-business is about more than technology jobs. In fact, e-commerce creates traditional jobs in logistics, call centres, warehousing, and trucking in far greater numbers than it creates IT jobs. All parts of our economy stand to gain by embracing e-business. Our e-business performance will have a growing impact on employment, sales, productivity, and investment throughout the economy. And it will result in efficiencies in all sectors, including government.

Five High-Yield Opportunities

How can we come together as a nation and a business community to tackle this opportunity? The Roundtable's agenda for 2001 focuses on five "high-yield" opportunities for moving Canada to the next level of e-business leadership:

- Make Canada a magnet for talent.
- Close the venture capital gap.
- Build Canada's international brand.
- Accelerate e-business adoption in small- and medium-sized businesses.
- Harness government on-line strategies and processes— increasingly known as GOL — as an e-business driver.

Let's take each in turn.

MAKE CANADA A MAGNET FOR TALENT

Senior Canadian executives have cited recruitment as their biggest e-business challenge. Canada needs to cultivate Internet-savvy executives, technologists, and the next generation of e-business talent. To ensure managers are Web savvy, we need to offer e-business skills training programs aimed at senior managers.

Creating a friendlier and more streamlined process for admitting skilled foreign workers to Canada would give us a much-needed edge over the United States in the war for scarce talent. Your government has started using immigration policy to attract highly skilled workers and speed up the processing. However, we are doing much less in this regard than other countries—especially in regions with large pools of potential technology emigrants such as India. Moving to expand the intake of New Economy workers further through this stream-lined process will also help attract foreign companies to invest in Canada as technology firms seek locations outside Silicon Valley, with its high real estate and service costs. And finally, Canada should be setting its own high standards for Internet education and working aggressively to implement them.

CLOSE THE VENTURE CAPITAL GAP

Access to early-stage, Internet-savvy, and participative venture capital is critical for the survival of budding e-businesses. To grow the venture capital pool in Canada, we must concentrate on three core drivers: increasing institutional investment, attracting foreign investment, and creating capital markets more favourable to technology initial public offerings (IPOs).

Institutional investors in Canada continue to under-invest in venture capital relative to their American counterparts. In 1999, U.S. pension funds contributed approximately $15.8 billion in new venture capital, representing 23% of new funds raised; meanwhile, Canadian pension funds contributed $134 million, representing only 5.6% of new funds raised.

If Canadian pension funds' venture capital asset allocations were at the same level as those in the United States, Canada's venture capital pool would more than double in size. If the proportion of new annual venture capital investment from pension funds matched that of the U.S., yearly contributions in Canada would rise from $134 million to over $600 million.

Venture capital investment could be stimulated if foreign content definitions and regulations were revised to accommodate Canadian venture capital financing structures. The government should also fully unblock the flow of foreign investment into venture capital funds by creating tax neutrality for non-resident investment in Canadian businesses. Fair treatment to protect foreign nontaxable investors in Canadian venture capital funds would significantly boost those funds' efforts to position Canada as an investment location of choice.

We also need to work to create more efficient capital markets for new economy IPOs. Canada hosted only six Internet-related IPOs in 2000 as compared to 128 on the NASDAQ stock market.

BUILD CANADA'S INTERNATIONAL BRAND

Perception and performance are inextricably linked. If Canada is perceived to be an e-business leader, it will attract investment and resources, and generate the entrepreneurial activity needed to increase e-business performance.

Canada established an early lead in developing a favourable legal and policy environment for e-business growth and investment. That was solidified last year by legislation providing for on-line privacy protection and for the use of digital signatures and records. Changes to federal tax policies have also greatly improved the fiscal environment for e-business. But we can't stop there.

Governments, like businesses, must be innovators. Canada has been at the vanguard of Internet public policy development and should work to maintain its reputation for progressive policy leadership.

Canada needs to rebuild its profile to increase investment in Canadian businesses by domestic and international investors. We need to encourage the development of a more entrepreneurial culture at home. The message we should be sending is that e-business is Canada's business. The government should be working with business to promote Canada's unique advantages, tell its New Economy success stories, and build its international reputation.

ACCELERATE E-BUSINESS ADOPTION IN SMALL- AND MEDIUM-SIZED BUSINESSES

Canada's small- and medium-sized companies, which account for 88% of national employment, are the collective core of a healthy economy. These companies need help in overcoming basic hurdles to Internet adoption and growth, including justifying the short-term costs and overcoming data security concerns.

Some of this can be done through the efforts of industry associations. However, governments can also play a role by providing businesses with "how-to" tools and information on best practices.

Harness Government On-Line Strategies and Processes as Drivers of E-Business

Getting the government's on-line practices right is important because it can increase efficiencies and reduce service costs for consumers, improve the speed and ease of basic business processes, pull other organizations on-line, and spur the development of domestic infrastructure to provide on-line services. This infrastructure can then be used in other parts of the Canadian economy and be exported to other markets.

Successful government on-line programs are often anchored in four factors that drive pace and performance: high-level leadership, aggressive targets and goal setting, measuring and reporting, and strategic investment.

Canada achieved early government on-line leadership; however, our governments are currently more focused on providing information than fully capitalizing on interaction or transaction capabilities. Other countries have launched major initiatives that could catapult them ahead of us. The U.K. is aiming to have 70% of government services available on-line by 2002 and 100% by 2005. Similarly, the goal of the U.K. government is to have 50% of tenders submitted electronically by December 2001 and 100% by December 2002.

The federal government has committed to putting all federal services on-line by 2004. That should happen sooner so that users, both individuals and businesses, can reap the benefits of more efficient and accessible service delivery. Unless all levels of government in Canada make on-line practices an urgent priority, we will go from leader to laggard.

Ten Years From Now: A Vision of What Could Be

If we are successful during the next year, our chances of being successful ten years from now will be that much greater. What might our success look like in 10 years? The answer to that futuristic question turns out to be the reason why leadership today, in the second inning of the game, is so critical.

In ten years, there will be no so-called new economy businesses. All parts of our economy will be making e-business their business. Canada will lead the world in prosperity. Canada will have emerged as a global e-business leader, having maintained 5% of global Internet economy revenue, and confirmed its reputation as the most e-business-friendly environment in the world. Our high-tech sector will have enabled us to sustain GDP growth of 4%, having exceeded forecasts and surpassed the OECD average of 2.5%. Unemployment will have been reduced to 5% versus the OECD average of 7%. This prosperity will have translated into a substantially improved Canadian standard of living.

Within Canada, a start-up culture akin to Silicon Valley's heyday will have emerged. Clusters in Ottawa-Montreal, Toronto-Waterloo, Vancouver-Seattle, and Calgary-Edmonton will have become hotbeds of innovation. A number of present-day Canadian mid-cap, high-tech companies will have graduated to global status, and a multitude of new mid-caps will have formed in high-growth subsectors such as bio-informatics, digital customer relationship management, and health care data services. Canada will also have become a major exporter of digital content, building on its strong film and multimedia presence.

Several of our largest high-tech companies will have become major multinationals that keep most of their jobs in Canada because of what has become known around the world as the "Canadian advantage"—a combination of factors that includes our high quality of life, superior education, and health care services, and cultural amenities. Canada will be, and be seen as, one of the most competitive and attractive business environments in the world.

Traditional Canadian industries will have become global leaders in the adoption of new technologies. Canada's mining industry will lead its global peers in the digitization of global geological surveys into searchable databases that can be easily updated. The health care industry will become a centre for patient population research and database management, leveraging Canada's leadership as home to the world's largest continuous databases of health care information. Finally, Canada will have become a global leader in Internet-based distance learning, spawning a new industry in which we dominate the market.

The "brain drain" will have been reversed so that there is more talent flowing into Canada than seeping out. Personal income taxes will be comparable to those in the United States, and capital gains taxes will have been eliminated altogether. Canada will be a magnet for talent from around the world, and many foreign multinationals from countries like India and China will have established their North American headquarters or major development labs in Canada. Our centres of excellence and advanced education institutions will have helped draw these minds, ideas, and innovation centres into Canada.

Canada's venture capital industry will have blossomed to include several players equal in size to their major American counterparts, and numerous global venture capital firms will have established operations here. Canadian pension funds will have dramatically increased their allocation to venture capital, helping to drive dramatic growth in our venture capital pool. Many Canadian expatriate entrepreneurs will have returned from the United States to become angel investors, venture capitalists, and mentors to budding enterprises.

Canadian governments at all levels will have become models of how to implement new technologies to improve services and reduce costs. In the process, Canada's procurement efforts will have helped to create Canadian companies that export these new products and services globally.

The rollout of broadband network infrastructure will have put the Internet at the fingertips of every community, business, and individual in Canada, allowing them to participate in and contribute to the Internet economy. Canada's not-for-profit sector will have also become an e-business leader, as on-line charitable giving will have dramatically reduced costs and increased giving.

Canadian schools will have become totally interconnected. Young people across Canada will be excited to be part of a country that leads the world in technology and opportunity. They will be more comfortable with technology than their international counterparts and will see entrepreneurship as an exciting career choice.

Our leadership in the Internet economy will be recognized worldwide and be a source of pride among Canadians at home and abroad.

John Loxley

John Loxley | *is a professor and former head of economics at the University of Manitoba and serves as an advisor to that province's minister of finance and as an economic consultant to* the Credit Union Central of Manitoba. He was the founding chair of CHO!CES, a coalition for social justice, and until this year co-coordinated the preparation of the Alternative Federal Budget, which shows different policy measures from those favoured in Ottawa and business circles. He has lived and worked in a number of developing countries and is currently the chairman of the board of directors of the North-South Institute in Ottawa. His publications include *Debt and Disorder: Finance for External Development* and *Interdependence, Disequilibrium and Growth: Reflections on the Political Economy of North-South Relations at the Turn of the Century.*

UNIVERSITY
OF MANITOBA | Department of Economics

John Loxley
Professor of Economics,
University of Manitoba

Winnipeg, Manitoba
Canada   R3T 5V5
telephone (204) 474-9207
facsimile (204) 474-7681
economics@umanitoba.ca

M E M O R A N D U M

To: **The Prime Minister of Canada**

From: **John Loxley** | *Professor of Economics,*
University of Manitoba

Subject: **Fixing Fiscal Policy**

The Liberal government may have thought that the pre-election mini-budget in the fall of 2000 would put an end to the debate about how best to use fiscal surpluses in Canada. In opting for the largest tax reductions in living memory, the Liberals effectively cut the electoral ground from underneath the Alliance, their major political threat, and easily secured another term in office. In principle, fiscal policy has now been set until the middle of the decade, as spending and tax plans extend out to 2005-06.

The Alliance has raised the question of the viability of those projections in the event of a recession in the coming years. The government has argued that sufficient flexibility is built into existing targets to safeguard against a mere slowing down of the economy. That is undoubtedly correct. The 2000 mini-budget has a $3-billion contingency reserve built into it and provision for "economic prudence" of $1 billion for 2001–02, rising each year thereafter to $4 billion by 2005–06. That, together with falls in interest rates (and, therefore, costs of servicing public debt) that inevitably accompany an economic slowdown, would protect against growth slipping by two to three percentage points a year. Only a major and prolonged recession of the Canadian economy is likely to seriously throw out last year's projections.

Changes in federal policy since 1995, however, have rendered ordinary Canadians much more vulnerable to even an economic slowdown (let alone a recession) than they were previously. Provincial budgets are also now much more susceptible to a recession than is the federal budget. Recent tax changes also raise important issues of equity, whatever happens to growth in the economy. For those reasons the government should revisit fiscal policy, and should do so sooner rather than later.

The most important changes in federal fiscal policy that are needed are the following:

- The balance between tax cuts and expenditure increases should be revisited.
- The Canada Health and Social Transfer should be further enhanced and reformed to reintroduce cost sharing of social assistance support.
- Employment Insurance benefits should be raised to widen and deepen the level of support for Canadians who lose their jobs.
- The Equalization program should be reformed to increase support to "have-not" provinces.
- Public spending on infrastructure and housing should be enhanced.
- A much more concerted effort should be made to implement the recommendations of the Royal Commission on Aboriginal Peoples.
- Announced tax cuts should be rescinded in favour of more targeted tax cuts for the poor.

Let's look at that plan in more detail:

1. Tax Cuts and Debt Reduction or Expenditure Increases

Recent fiscal policy has been heavily weighted toward tax cuts and debt reduction. Cumulatively, tax cuts account for about

45% of fiscal initiatives between 1997–98 and 2002–03, debt reduction for 17%, and spending initiatives for 38%. Policy decisions taken in the two budgets of 2000 will cost $29 billion between 1999–00 and 2002–03, excluding debt reduction, and fully 65% of that will take the form of tax reductions, with only 35% coming from spending increases. In addition, should the contingency provision not be needed, it will be applied to debt reduction.

The problem with those proportions is that the federal budget was balanced over the 1994 to 1999 period largely by massive cuts to program spending. Over that period, spending cutbacks explain 62% of budgetary "improvement," lower interest rates 19%, and increased taxation from economic growth 19%, according to a Canadian Auto Workers Union study. Between 1992 and 1999, program spending as a share of GDP fell by 9.5 percentage points to under 12% of GDP, constituting, as Paul Martin likes to boast, "a greater reduction than in any other G-7 country." Those cuts brought spending to its lowest level as a percentage of GDP since 1949-50. Even after recent spending initiatives, program spending will not exceed 11.4% of GDP in 2002-03.

Given the unmet demands for public services, the emphasis in fiscal policy should be on enhanced government spending rather than tax and debt reduction. That is particularly so when the economy slows, since spending is much more effective than tax reduction as a counter-cyclical device. The reality is that steady economic growth is all that is needed to reduce the debt-to-GDP ratio.

2. The Canada Health and Social Transfer

The introduction of the Canada Health and Social Transfer in 1995 was essentially a cost-cutting measure. The two transfers it replaced, the Canada Assistance Plan and the Established Programs Financing for Health and Education, provided substantially more in total than the Canada Health and Social Transfer when it was first introduced. Moreover, the Canada

Assistance Plan had been designed to cover 50% of social assistance costs incurred by provinces, although that had been eroded for provinces not drawing on Equalization. While the election budget of October 2000 went a long way toward reinstating transfers for health care spending, it did not go all the way and it did not compensate provinces for health transfers lost after 1995–96. It made no attempt to reinstate transfers for postsecondary education to previous levels. Above all, nothing was done to reinstate cost sharing of social assistance payments—leaving provinces to foot the bill entirely in the next economic downturn. That will render less well-off provinces particularly vulnerable to recession.

Accepting that the federal government is unlikely to reintroduce full cost sharing, perhaps a compromise could be reached. In recognition of stubbornly high rates of poverty, despite relative economic prosperity, it could offer to cost-share an improvement to social assistance rates, which have been cut substantially across the country since 1995–96 and to cost-share any increase in the number of people relying on social assistance in the event of an economic downturn. That would help buffer provinces at the margin.

3. Employment Insurance

Improvements to social assistance need to be accompanied by improving the eligibility for unemployment insurance (now euphemistically termed "employment" insurance). As a result of cuts throughout the 1990s, less than a third of unemployed workers are now eligible to draw Employment Insurance. The stage is thus set for an income crisis for the unemployed in the next recession and for a fiscal disaster for the provinces, as workers who would have had the protection of unemployment insurance in the last recession have to rely more heavily on welfare. The government should revisit its plans to cut Employment Insurance premiums and put the money, instead, into improved benefits, reducing qualifying time, improving rates, and lengthening the eligibility period.

4. Equalization

In fiscal year 2000, the federal government removed the Equalization ceiling, set at $10 billion, effectively increasing payments by $0.8 billion. The ceiling is now back in place and have-not provinces are beginning to feel the pinch as the differential growth rates between them and better-off provinces widen and as this important source of revenue becomes completely income-inelastic. The federal government is reluctant to remove the ceiling mainly because over 45% of all payments flow to Quebec, and Premier Bernard Landry has been particularly ungrateful for enhanced Equalization flows, describing a recent $1.5-billion windfall as evidence of Quebec's humiliation. But the needs of the poorer provinces are real, as they struggle to cope with increasing costs of service delivery.

The other reform needed in Equalization is to the five-province standard on which payments are calculated. Provinces receive Equalization if their revenue-raising capacity is below that of five, "middle income" provinces that make up the standard: Quebec, Ontario, Manitoba, Saskatchewan, and British Columbia. With the increase in oil revenues, Alberta's fiscal capacity is now over $10,000 per person compared with the "standard" of $5,914 for 2000-01. A strong case can be made for including Alberta in the standard or for a reversion to a ten-province standard, which would enhance payments to poorer provinces.

Should increases in Equalization be unacceptable politically, the federal government should consider making special payments to smaller "have-not" provinces to allow them to improve services, on the argument that being so small they lack economies of scale, which increases their per-capita cost of service delivery, even after wage differentials are allowed for.

5. Housing and Infrastructure

Homelessness continues to be a major problem in Canada, as does inner-city housing decay. Canada is also currently running huge infrastructure deficits, in highways, water treatment and environmental improvement, and energy conservation. Those would be ideal areas in which public spending could increase as the economy slows since they are labour intensive, can be balanced regionally, and have lasting social value.

6. *The Royal Commission on Aboriginal Peoples*

The Royal Commission on Aboriginal Peoples called for increasing government spending to address the multifaceted problems facing Aboriginal peoples, which have been aptly described as "Canada's shame" by John McCallum, the ex-Royal Bank economist elected as a Liberal MP. Spending would rise initially, by as much as $1.5 to $2 billion per year but would lead to improvements in Aboriginal living standards that would eventually reduce total net government spending on Aboriginal affairs. There is no doubt that the government could afford to implement those recommendations if it wished, yet to date increases in government spending have been modest, amounting to maybe $270 million a year by 2003, with 40% going to health. A much greater emphasis needs to be put on economic development and labour-force training initiatives than is currently the case and recent controversies over the accountability of Aboriginal leaders should not be seized upon as an excuse not to do so.

7. *Taxation*

The tax reduction measures announced by the government in the 2000 mini-budget disproportionately benefit the rich in Canada. The top third of taxpayers will get 83% of the announced income tax cuts—the richest 5% pull in almost 40%—while the poorest third will enjoy only 4% of the benefits, according to a study by Hugh Mackenzie for the Canadian Centre for Policy Alternatives. That is the logic of focusing tax cuts on capital gains taxes, high-income surtaxes, and larger absolute cuts in tax rates on higher incomes. Low-income earners, it is true, have benefited from earlier tax cuts, mainly in the form of abolition of the low-income surtax and enhancement of child tax benefits, though the latter were not passed on to people on social assistance. But poverty, even among those with jobs, remains unacceptably high. Any further tax cuts, after allowing for the spending measures outlined earlier, should therefore be concentrated on low- and middle-income groups.

By moving to a tax-on-income system, away from setting their taxes as an automatic percentage of federal taxes, provinces have insulated themselves from having to automatically pass on further tax cuts in response to federal cuts. Now, as Alberta threatens to use its huge revenue capacity to lower personal and business taxes, it is putting pressure on other provinces to compete when many simply do not have the resources to do so. This is yet another reason why Equalization payments should be adjusted to reflect Alberta's huge revenue advantage.

Conclusion

It may be thought that the last election settled, once and for all, how the fiscal surplus will be spent. But many fiscal policy decisions taken since 1995 have had adverse social and perhaps even constitutional implications. Those problems will not disappear simply because a budget plan seemed to have strong electoral support. That plan did not address the implications for both individuals and provinces of a possible recession. It did not reverse previous cuts in social transfers and programs and it did not address, adequately, a number of very pressing social problems in Canada, especially those facing Aboriginal people. Its tax cuts were heavily targeted toward higher income groups. The government can expect pressure in the coming years to reorient its fiscal polices along the lines suggested here.

Jason Clemens
and Joel Emes

Jason Clemens | *is director of fiscal studies and nonprofit studies at the Fraser Institute.* He is also the coordinator of the *Survey of Investment Managers*, a quarterly survey summarizing the views and opinions of Canada's largest institutional investors on public policy issues. He has an Honours Bachelor's degree in commerce and a Master's degree in business administration from the University of Windsor, as well as a Post-Baccalaureate Diploma in economics from Simon Fraser University. He is currently working on his second Master's degree in public policy at Simon Fraser University.

Joel Emes | *is senior research economist at the Fraser Institute.* He received his M.A. in economics from Simon Fraser University. He is a regular contributor to The Fraser Institute's monthly magazine *Fraser Forum* and is co-author of *Tax Facts 10* and *Canada's All Government Debt*. Mr. Emes is also the primary researcher for Tax Freedom Day and the institute's provincial and state-provincial fiscal comparisons, the Budget Performance Index, and the Fiscal Performance Index.

They are the co-authors of the Fraser Institute's recent study *Flat Tax: Issues and Principles*, available on the Internet at www.fraserinstitute.ca.

Offering market solutions
to public policy problems
since 1974.

HEAD OFFICE:
4th Floor, 1770 Burrard Street
Vancouver, British Columbia
Canada V6J 3G7
Phone: (604) 688-0221
Fax: (604) 688-8539
Web site:
   www.fraserinstitute.ca
E-mail:
   info@fraserinstitute.ca

TORONTO OFFICE:
Phone: (416) 363-6575
Fax: (416) 601-7322

OTTAWA OFFICE:
Phone: (603) 565-0468

CALGARY OFFICE:
301 – 815 1st Street S.W.
Calgary, Alberta
Canada T2P 1N3
Phone: (403) 216-7175
Fax: (403) 234-9010

With strategic
alliances
in 53 countries.

MEMORANDUM

To: The Prime Minister of Canada

From: Jason Clemens and Joel Emes |
Analysts, *The Fraser Institute*

Subject: Flat Tax: A Viable Alternative

The issue of tax relief has overwhelmed the equally important issue of tax reform in the national debate. Unfortunately, the attention drawn to this issue during the last federal election was riddled with misinformation that effectively prevented an open and rational debate about tax reform in this country.

The traditional evaluation criteria for taxes are efficiency, fairness, and simplicity. Efficiency refers to the minimization of economic distortions—taxes shouldn't distort the economic activities that individuals and corporations would otherwise make. Fairness, or what is now referred to as equity, has two components. Horizontal equity requires that individuals with similar incomes face similar tax burdens. Vertical equity requires that individuals pay more tax as their incomes increase. Finally, simplicity refers to the level of comprehension and understanding of the tax system by citizens.

There is little disagreement that the current Canadian tax system fails to achieve any of the traditional measures of tax policy success. For instance, there are numerous tax credits designed to benefit narrow segments of the Canadian population that effectively distort economic decisions and create economic inefficiencies, thus violating the principle of efficiency. Similarly, the Canadian system is fraught with tax-based biases that contravene the principle of fairness. Finally, very few people would argue that the current system is readily understandable by citizens. Thus, there is an opportunity and indeed a need for fundamental reform of the Canadian system based on efficiency, fairness, and simplicity.

The Hall-Rabushka Proposal

When discussing a move to a flat tax, it is important to differentiate between a flat tax and the replacement of multiple tax rates with a single rate. The type of tax reform implemented in Alberta this year and proposed by the Canadian Alliance in the recent federal election was actually that second option: the replacement of multiple tax rates with a single rate. That is actually but one step in the process of broad-based flat tax reform.

There are a number of prominent flat tax proposals. The most discussed was developed by Robert E. Hall and Alvin Rabushka of the Hoover Institution. It taxes all types of income once and at one tax rate. In their most recent analysis, in 1995, Hall and Rabushka recommended replacing the five personal federal income tax rates in the United States (15%, 28%, 31%, 36%, and 39.6%) and the various business tax rates with a 19% federal tax rate for all types of income earned by individuals and businesses.

The Hall-Rabushka proposal contains no tax credits, deductions, or exemptions except for the personal, spousal, and child exemptions. In other words, the myriad of tax breaks present in the current system and the accompanying complicated and time-consuming paperwork are eliminated. Further, flat tax reform significantly simplifies the determination of income, which constitutes much of the complexity associated with the current tax system. The Hall-Rabushka proposal clearly achieves one of the core criteria of tax policy, namely simplicity.

Hall and Rabushka take an integrated approach to taxation in which both business income and personal income are taxed once and only once. As a result of that uniform taxation coupled with the presence of a personal exemption, the flat tax achieves both vertical and horizontal equity. Individuals with similar incomes face similar tax burdens, which is horizontal equity, and individuals pay more taxes as their income increases, which is vertical equity. Another benefit of the Hall-Rabushka proposal is that it effectively moves the income tax system away from a system based on income towards one based on consumption. A consumption tax is levied on any income that in turn is consumed—spent rather than saved. The Hall-Rabushka proposal excludes savings and investment from taxation, which effectively creates a tax system based on taxing consumption rather than income. That achieves the third of the tax criteria, efficiency. Economists generally agree that taxation of consumption is one of the most efficient manners in which to raise tax revenue, because it minimizes distortions.

There are also a number of important macroeconomic benefits from the Hall-Rabushka idea, such as improved incentives for work, increased entrepreneurial activity, and greater capital formation leading to higher levels of national output and increases in the standard of living.

Progressivity: Why We Have Multiple Rates

Progressivity is the principle that taxpayers should pay more income tax as a percentage of their income as they earn more. That has been achieved, traditionally, using progressively higher income tax rates applied on progressively higher earnings.

But evidence regarding the negative effects of high and increasing marginal tax rates is robust and growing. A number of major economic studies concluded in the last two decades that high and increasing marginal tax rates have negative effects on rates of economic growth. Further, a 1998 study by Robert Carroll, Douglas Holtz-Eakin, Mark Rider, and Harvey S. Rosen,

Entrepreneurs, Income Taxes and Investment, found that higher marginal tax rates reduce capital formation, a key ingredient to long-term economic growth. In general, there is ample evidence that high and increasing marginal tax rates contribute to lower rates of economic growth, reduced rates of personal income growth, lower rates of capital formation and investment, lower than expected aggregate labour supply, and reduced social welfare. In short, high and increasing marginal tax rates reduce economic growth by creating strong disincentives to hard work, savings, and investment.

Flat Tax Case Calculations

One of the many benefits associated with a flat tax is that it is able to achieve progressivity in the tax system—those earning more pay more in taxes as a percentage of their income—while at the same time eliminating the damaging effects of high and increasing marginal tax rates. That is achieved by including a personal exemption in the flat tax. Since a portion of income is exempt from tax, someone who earns $100,000 would pay more tax, both nominally and as a percentage of income than someone earning less.

In our recent study for the Fraser Institute, *Flat Tax: Issues and Principles*, we created nine separate flat taxes using Statistics Canada's Social Policy Simulation Database and Model with 2000 as a base tax year. Unfortunately, due to limitations within that database, we were able to model only personal income tax reform. The flat taxes in the accompanying chart range from a simple system with no exemptions or deductions to a system with generous individual and spousal exemptions, child exemptions, full RRSP and RPP exemptions, and charitable donation deductibility. The first seven flat tax cases hold government revenue constant—there is no reduction in the amount of revenue collected by the federal or provincial governments. Cases eight and nine reduce the amount of revenues collected by the federal government.

Flat Tax Case	Value of Personal and Spousal Exemption	Value of Child-care Exemption	Change in Revenue Collected*	Deduction for RRSP/RPP**	Deduction for Charitable Donations**	Federal Flat Tax Rate, %	Weighted Provincial Average Flat Tax Rate, %	Ontario Provincial Flat Tax Rate, *** %
1	$0	$0	$0	No	No	12.7	7.0	5.8
2	$7,231	$0	$0	No	No	16.7	9.4	7.5
3	$8,766	$0	$0	No	No	17.8	10.0	7.9
4	$17,532	$0	$0	No	No	26.1	14.8	11.2
5	$8,766	$2,000	$0	No	No	18.3	10.3	8.1
6	$8,766	$2,000	$0	Yes	No	19.9	11.1	8.8
7	$8,766	$2,000	$0	Yes	Yes	20.1	11.2	8.9
8	$11,834	$2,000	-$13.4	Yes	No	19.0	12.9	10.0
9	$11,834	$2,000	-$22.3	Yes	No	16.5	12.9	10.0

* Refers to the Federal Government only. Any change in the amount of revenue collected implies an expenditure and tax reduction at the federal level only. Stated in billions of dollars.
** RRSP/RPP contributions and charitable donations, if present, are treated as they currently exist in the tax system.
*** Presented for illustrative purposes only.

The value of the personal exemption has an enormous influence on the applicable flat tax rates. The larger the personal exemption, the higher the applicable flat tax rate. There is, therefore, a powerful tradeoff between the value of the personal (and spousal) exemption and the applicable tax rate.

Income Dynamics and Mobility

The most often-cited criticism levied against flat taxes is that they dramatically shift the burden of taxation from high-income earners to low- and middle-income earners. To a certain extent that shift in the tax burden is inevitable given the extremely progressive nature of Canada's tax system. For instance, the Fraser Institute's recent book on taxation, *Tax Facts 12*, indicates that the top 13% of tax-filers—those earning in excess of $50,000 per year—earned 40.7% of all the income declared to Revenue Canada for tax purposes but contributed 59.5% of personal income taxes paid.

The criticism is significantly diminished, however, when one considers the high degree of income mobility in Canada. Individual and household incomes don't remain constant over time, as some of the critics of flat taxes seem to assume. There is a life-cycle structure to incomes in which earnings tend to increase as individuals age, up to a certain stage —normally retirement—at which point they decline. A recent study found that over a two-year period 13.8% of households moved up one quintile in the income distribution while an additional 3.2% moved up more than one quintile. Of those households initially in the bottom two quintiles in 1995, 24% found themselves at least one quintile higher by 1996. Indeed, over a five-year period, according to another study, a total of 45% of those in the bottom two quintiles moved up at least one quintile.

The ability of individuals and households to move up the income spectrum demands that longer time horizons be incorporated in tax analysis in order to determine the real, long-term effect of tax policy. Such a long-term analysis strongly suggests that individuals would gain under any of the nine flat tax proposals we presented, as any initial tax increase would be more than offset by later tax reductions during the individual's peak earning period.

Conclusion

The fairest, most efficient, and simplest tax system upon which to base reform of the Canadian tax system is a flat tax model based on the work of Hall and Rabushka. Such a system would provide enormous positive incentives for hard work, savings, and investment. The evidence suggests economic benefits of implementing a flat tax system would include greater rates of economic and income growth, higher levels of capital formation and investment, and greater social welfare.

The tax system would not, as many argue, have to relinquish the principle of progressivity. Rather, a flat tax system that includes a personal exemption would enable Canada to maintain progressivity while bypassing the costs of high and increasing marginal tax rates. Viewing such reform over the course of one's life rather than within a single year also indicates that nearly all taxpayers would gain from such a reform.

In short, a flat tax system presents enormous economic benefits with few economic costs. The Hall-Rabushka flat tax with its common rate for all types of income should be the model upon which Canada begins to discuss and ultimately design real tax reform.

Bruce O'Hara

Bruce O'Hara in 1984, while working as a counsellor, became concerned that most of his clients—indeed, most Canadians—were either unemployed or overworked. He founded Work Well, Canada's first work options resource centre, to facilitate better and more balanced ways to apportion work and was its executive director until 1990. He has written two books on the issue, *Put Work in Its Place* and *Working Harder Isn't Working*. Mr. O'Hara and his partner, Lynne, live in Courtenay, British Columbia, where he juggles a passion for gardening and outdoor pleasures with various writing projects, stress reduction workshops, public speaking, and workplace consulting.

ECONOMIC
CANADA

BRUCE O'HARA

Bruce O'Hara
Consultant on Stress and Workplace Issues

379 Third Street
Courtenay, British Columbia
V9N 1E3
Tel: (205) 335-0949
e-mail: boh@mars.ark.com

To: **The Prime Minister of Canada**

From: **Bruce O'Hara** | *Consultant on stress and workplace issues*

Subject: **Europe's Big Shift on Work Hours**

Europe is in the midst of a revolution in working time. It's a revolution with major implications for Canada's future.

Europeans now work hundreds of hours per year less than their Canadian counterparts. The main benefit of working less, as far as they're concerned, has been an enormous increase in the quality of family and community life. Europeans can point to a whole slew of public health and child welfare indicators showing that Europe is a far healthier place to raise families than North America is.

The impacts on unemployment are far from trivial, though. In the past two years, by moving from a 39 to a 35-hour workweek, France has put one-third of its unemployed back to work. As a result, business confidence in France has risen to an all-time high. Holland, Norway, and Sweden have combined modest reductions in the standard workweek with big expansions in voluntary part-time work, to drive unemployment rates down below 3%.

Europe has been reducing work times long enough to develop some solid cost parameters in relation to the tradeoffs involved. First, there are productivity gains. Workers on shorter workweeks are fresher: They get more done per hour and make fewer mistakes. It's a rule of thumb that one-third of any work-time reduction will be offset by higher productivity.

Shorter workweeks spread the same work among more workers. Each person who comes off welfare or unemployment insurance saves the government purse about $15,000 a year. It's a reliable rule of thumb that those savings to government work out to be the equivalent of about one-third of the loss in wages that workers would otherwise expect as a result of working fewer hours. Finally, because shorter work times in Europe have been pursued as a quality-of-life measure, workers have usually been willing to chip in about a third of the cost of working less. So, for example, when a company moves from a thirty-five- to a thirty-two-hour workweek, what's happening is that workers get paid for thirty-four hours, government rebates to the employer the equivalent of an hour's wages in the form of payroll tax reductions, and the employer recoups the remaining hour through higher productivity.

Why aren't similar changes happening here? It's not because Canadians don't want to work less. In poll after poll, Canadians are saying that they are stressed out and need more time off. Major unions such as the Canadian Auto Workers and the Communications, Energy and Paperworkers Union have been bargaining for work-time reductions. And you don't need to tell Canadian employers that a tired and stressed-out work force is less than productive, makes too many mistakes, and is cranky with the customers. They see it every day.

Rewarding Overwork in Canada

So why has Canada been moving in the opposite direction—to longer workweeks and more overtime? I won't mince words, Prime Minister: The federal government is the problem. You haven't been paying attention. Where Europe has adjusted its payroll tax structure to reward employers who create jobs and punish employers who destroy jobs, Canada has left in place an antiquated payroll tax and benefit structure that does exactly the opposite.

In Canada, employers who overwork their employees are rewarded with lower payroll taxes and reduced benefit costs. Employers who share the work and hire new employees? They pay more.

Payroll taxes and fixed benefit costs give rise to a dog-in-the-manger attitude, making Canadian employers resistant to voluntary, individual reductions in work time. The extra payroll costs an employer has to pay when an employee drops back to part-time work aren't quite as large as the savings an employer can expect through higher productivity. But those costs are visible and certain, while the productivity savings are hidden—and theoretical—in an employer's mind. They're enough to block good changes while encouraging bad ones.

The changes needed to reverse the onus of Canada's tax and benefit structure are relatively simple. First, restructure payroll deductions for Canada Pension Plan and Employment Insurance to make contribution rates zero on the first $8,000 of income per year. Remove the ceilings on contributory income at the same time. Taken together, the two changes are revenue-neutral, so Canada Pension Plan and Employment Insurance benefits can remain as they are. The $8,000 exemption means that proportionately more of a part-timer's wages are payroll-tax free—making them cheaper on a cost-per-hour basis. (It also makes summer students more attractive and reduces the tax burden of low-income workers at the same time.) Removing the ceilings on payroll taxes means that longer work hours become more expensive: At overtime rates, employers would pay time-and-a-half on payroll taxes too.

The other area needing reform is health care benefits. As currently structured, medical and dental plans are a large and fixed cost for employers. When employees work overtime, the cost per hour of those benefits goes down. When the workweek is shortened, costs per hour rise. How should it be changed? A first step would be for the federal government to work with the provinces to expand medicare to include dental care coverage. Then, instead of funding medicare and denticare as a fixed fee item, it should be funded as a contributory program like the Canada Pension Plan and Employment Insurance, with a zero contribution rate on the first $8,000 of income and a percentage rate contribution on all income thereafter.

With those changes in place, the perverse rewards of the current system would be reversed: Employers who overwork their employees would bear the cost of the unemployment they create. Employers who spread the work around would share in the savings that result when welfare and Employment Insurance costs are reduced. There's no need to legislate a shorter workweek. Just remove the obstacles that have prevented the three million Canadians who want to work less from doing so, and they'll cut Canada's unemployment rate in half while making their work schedules more family-friendly.

The Two-Shift Society: Creating Two Weekends

I think you should also know that the changes in Europe we've seen so far are only a prologue to what I believe is on the way. To date, work-time reductions in Europe have taken place as a series of small steps that haven't changed the basic structure of the workplace. Employers and unions have now hit an impasse, which is pushing Europe to look at a big shift in how work is organized.

Employers have been complaining that overhead costs per workstation go up if you shorten the workweek and leave plant and equipment idle more of the week. On the other hand, if making the standard workweek shorter makes the weekend shift long enough to provide a livable income, and a weekend shift is hired, then shorter workweeks can lead to plant and equipment being used seven days a week, and big savings in overhead costs. Equally important, shorter workweeks can reduce or increase the hours of service a business is able to offer, depending on whether a single- or multiple-shift model is used.

In capital-intensive industries, work-time reduction on a multiple-shift model can reduce overhead costs by an amount equivalent to one-half of the wage reduction that employees would expect to face working fewer hours. Shorter workweeks on a single-shift model can increase an employer's costs by an equally large factor. So business is digging in its heels and saying, "No more work-time reductions unless they're structured so as to reduce overhead costs." Unions, on the other hand, are saying that there's already too much weekend work, and they've reached the limit of what they'll allow.

Finding ways around that standoff is now the centre of the work-time debate. Finland has been running a series of experiments where the workday is divided into two six-hour shifts. Hours of service are increased and overhead costs go down. Workers get eight hours' pay for six hours' work, but between increases in productivity and decreases in overhead costs, employers feel that they're at least breaking even. Shop clerks in Holland now work four days a week, in three interlocking shifts that provide balanced coverage over a six-day retail week.

The result of such experiments is that Europe is now starting to look seriously at redesigning not just individual workplaces but the whole economy to run on two shifts. What would it be like if the entire workforce was split into two shifts that worked opposite ends of the week? Each shift would tag-team with the other, working three days one week and four the next, an average of 28 hours a week. Schools would go on the same two shifts. Almost everyone could work the same days their spouses worked and the same days that their kids went to school. Maybe the win-win way to eliminate weekend work is simply to create two weekends.

Advocates for a two-shift workforce point out that it's not just business that would benefit from reduced overhead costs. Run schools and government services on two shifts and you need fewer, smaller facilities. If only half the workforce is commuting to work on any given day you need fewer new highways and subways. Those extra savings would mean governments could increase their contribution to the cost of working less from one-third to a half, and still save money over all.

The extra savings inherent in a two-shift model are so large that business, with government's help, could offer a shorter workweek with no loss in pay, and save money while doing so. While a twenty-eight-hour workweek sounds implausibly short to North American ears, Prime Minister, it represents a reduction in working time of less than 10% to most European countries.

The work-time issue has had so much attention in Europe that my guess is that sometime in the next five years, at least one city or region will pilot-test a twenty-eight-hour workweek built around two community-wide shifts. I further predict that the model is so practical that it will quickly become the norm across Europe.

Eventually, we in Canada will be pushed into making the big shift to a 28-hour workweek. A shorthand way to think about why is to imagine that Canada and Holland are competing for the gold medal in hockey at the 2006 Winter Olympic Games. Team Canada puts six players on the ice and says to its team, "We want you to show your commitment to the team by really giving us your all." Those six players play the whole game, right through, with no breaks. Meanwhile, Team Holland has two six-person lines. They rotate every five minutes. They say to their team, "We want you to be fresh, so you can do your best, every minute you're on the ice." Who's going to win the gold?

Do we want to begin the twenty-first century playing catch-up to Europe's better idea? I think not. It's not like you need to do anything large or draconian. The federal government has only to remove the roadblocks it has created, and Canadians will find their own ways to the Promised Land of leisure.

It's happening, Prime Minister. That Age of Leisure and Prosperity futurists have so long predicted is finally happening. Only in Europe, you say? Pity.

SOCIAL
CANADA

Judith Maxwell

Bob Rae

Raisa Deber

Steven Lewis

Peter Holle

Dr. Nancy Olivieri

Margaret Hillyard Little

Fred McMahon

Jack Layton

Roger L. Martin

Gail Bowen

Allan Blakeney

Robert Hornung

Rick Findlay

Laura Jones

Part Three

Judith Maxwell

Judith Maxwell | *is president of the Canadian Policy Research Networks*, a new kind of think tank she founded in 1995 based on networks of researchers and policy advisors who focus on health, the family, and work. Mrs. Maxwell was chair of the Economic Council of Canada from 1985 to 1992, and prior to that worked as a consultant, as director of policy studies at the C.D. Howe Institute, and as a journalist. She is an adjunct professor at the University of Ottawa and a fellow of the School of Policy Studies at Queen's University. She is a member of the board of directors of BCE Inc. and Clarica, among others, and has been awarded honorary degrees by seven Canadian universities.

CPRN RCRPP

Canadian Policy Research Networks Inc.
Les réseaux canadiens de recherche en politiques publiques inc.

600-250 Albert Ottawa Ontario Canada K1P 6M1
📞 (613) 567-7500 ✉ (613) 567-7640 💻 www.cprn.org / www.rcrpp.org

MEMORANDUM

To: **The Prime Minister of Canada**

From: **Judith Maxwell** | *President,*
Canadian Policy Research Networks

Subject: **Room to Manoeuvre on Social Policy**

Canada's scope for making choices on economic and social policies far surpasses that of the 1990s.

How could that be you might ask, in the era of globalization? First of all, borders still do matter for the way in which people construct their lives. Provincial borders here in Canada permit wide variations in tax and social policies, between, for example, Ontario and Quebec, or Alberta and Saskatchewan. Even greater variations occur between states in the United States. Thus, the wonders of communications technology and the power of trade laws do not paint everyone the same colour.

But why is there more room to manoeuvre now than ten years ago? The main difference is that Canada has put its own economic house in better order. Government finances, inflation and interest rates, and corporate balance sheets have all shown dramatic improvements. That means Canada has earned more credibility in world financial markets, and with that credibility goes greater economic sovereignty.

Thus, the big argument should be about what we want to do with our newfound scope for making our own decisions. What challenges require major policy decisions in the 2000s?

Canadians have changed a great deal over the past twenty years. For example, we have accepted, even embraced, new rules for economic success. We rely much more on markets to determine how income will be distributed, where investments will be made, and who will be the winners and losers from economic change.

We are also a more diverse country, thanks to the continuing flow of immigration, and we are more pluralistic. Canadians do not defer to authority the way they used to. Opinion on key issues is more varied—with stronger voices on the right side of the political spectrum than we have seen in the past.

The hard times of the past twenty years have led to an erosion of our social protections. In general, employers offer less security to workers than they used to. Most families now have two wage earners and cannot afford to keep one adult at home to manage the care and nurturing of family members. Social transfers and services are now more targeted to particular groups. The middle class has been losing once-cherished benefits of universal programming, and more people are earning low and modest incomes. In all these ways, Canadians are now carrying more risk and are more vulnerable to market downturns.

Out of that situation, I see two major goals for economic and social policies. First, they should focus on maintaining and expanding Canada's room to manoeuvre; and second, they should be making a major effort to create a more durable synergy between the economic and the social. Canadians do not live to work, nor do they work to live. Their focus is on building a good quality of life for themselves and their children, now and in the future. That quality of life will embrace both the economic and the social.

Canada and the United States: The Room to Manoeuvre

When policy wonks gather to talk policy, there are always some voices in the room arguing that Canada should be more like the

United States. As North American integration proceeds, they seek a "level playing field"—with, for example, similar tax rates and freedom of choice for health care services.

In making such arguments, they grossly oversimplify the policy challenge. On some core issues, like the taxes on corporate and business income, Canada does have to match the United States, point for point. But that is not the case for taxes on personal income, where borders permit variation. So Canada has the scope to levy somewhat higher personal income taxes and to set a progressive rate structure, if it chooses.

The scope for constructing a positive role for government can also be expanded if Canada pays down its huge public debt at a faster pace. If we look at the composition of government spending in the two countries, it is clear that Canada spends far more money on interest on the public debt (an extra five percentage points of GDP in 1994, the last year for which I was able to obtain figures). As debt-servicing costs fall, Canada will free up more room to manoeuvre—more room to design uniquely Canadian responses to social and economic challenges.

A More Durable Synergy

From 1945 to the mid-1970s, federal and provincial governments achieved a strong synergy between the economic and social. By investing in education, health care, family allowances, housing, and industrial development, they fostered robust economic growth and gave Canadian citizens the tools and protections they needed to prosper. Throughout that period, economic growth was strong, standards of living improved, and income inequality declined. The pie got bigger and it was distributed more evenly.

Over the past twenty years, growth has been weak, per capita income after tax and after inflation has barely increased, and inequality has increased. The pie stopped growing, and the market distributed it unevenly. As Canada struggled with all its economic problems, economic priorities trumped the social. We lost the synergy created when the two were working together.

We learned in the postwar years that investments in access to education, health care, housing, and social services are actually investments in future self-reliance, which strongly reinforces economic growth. But the investments of the twenty-first century will be different from the welfare state of the twentieth century for the simple reason that work, family, and communities are different now.

Here are a few ideas for the new investments we could make in self-reliance—health care, learning, and social transfers. These are investments designed to buttress the strength of the economy.

HEALTH CARE

Investments in health in the postwar years were designed to protect families from personal bankruptcy caused by serious illness in the family. Today, Canadians have fairly universal access to hospital and medical care, although hospital stays are shorter, waiting lists are longer, and many districts lack doctors and nurses. Federal and provincial governments have begun to reinvest large sums of money in strengthening hospital and medical services to ensure that they will be able to meet citizens' needs. That includes round-the-clock primary care services to take the pressure off emergency rooms. Here there is scope for gains in effectiveness and efficiency, and to bolster confidence in both access and quality.

Another major focus should be on access to pharmaceuticals and community-based care. Access today is spotty. Some workers are insured through their employers. Most of the elderly and people on welfare are sometimes covered through government plans. But some people are going without. Others are digging deep into their own pockets to cover the cost by themselves. Yet drugs and home care have become the most effective substitutes for heavy use of hospital and medical services. Why should one group of services be universally available and the others not? Other industrialized countries provide insurance coverage for the full range of health services. Why not Canada?

LEARNING

Canada has created a universal public education system from kindergarten to the end of high school. But learning needs have changed in recent decades. We now know the importance of learning in the early years. Young people who do not continue their education after high school confront serious disadvantages in finding any job, let alone one that is well paid. And most adults, even the Ph.D.s and M.B.A.s, find that they need to keep renewing their skills throughout their lifetime.

So where should universal access to learning opportunities begin and end? Provinces have different views on the answer to that question. Quebec has recently introduced universal access to child care for pre-school children, at a rate of $5 a day, a fraction of the cost in other provinces. About two-thirds of young children in Canada have mothers who work full-time, but there are only regulated child care spaces in the other provinces for 10% to 15% of those children. Where do the others go while their parents work? And what kind of learning experiences do they get? How ready will they be to learn when they reach kindergarten?

Quebec and British Columbia continue to regulate university and college tuition fees to make those institutions accessible to a wider group of students. But the other provinces have removed the caps on tuition and cut operating grants to post-secondary institutions, leaving them no choice but to raise tuition fees and seek more funding from private sources. The net effect has been to impose a heavy financial burden on students and their families, make access dependent on ability to pay, and force a deterioration in university and college facilities.

All these things have happened at the same time that governments and employers preach the gospel of lifelong learning to prosper in the new knowledge-based economy. Certainly education brings significant benefits to individuals and they should be making a contribution to the cost. But education from birth to retirement also creates substantial benefits for society as a whole. Children who do well at school are far less likely to drop out or to get into trouble with the law or with substance abuse.

Adults who can upgrade their skills adapt more readily to chang-ing work conditions. Young people with excellent skills will bring the innovation and energy to make Canada a successful com-petitor in the world economy.

SOCIAL TRANSFERS

In Canada today, it is possible to have two full-time jobs at the minimum wage and not make enough money to support a family. It is possible to be employed full-time and not be able to find affordable housing. Homelessness in major cities afflicts more than drifters and street kids. It has spread to families with children. Poverty has become more concentrated in specific neighbourhoods in major cities.

The federal and provincial governments began to respond to child poverty in 1998. Working together, they have created the National Child Benefit, which combines a federal transfer to all families with children with provincial early childhood services. But the transfer still has not reached the level that reflects the costs of raising a child and the services are still patchy—excellent in some neighbourhoods, fragmented or nonexistent in others. A good beginning has been made but Canada has a long way to go to create a solid framework for healthy child development.

In the postwar period, the federal government created unemployment insurance to support adults who were tem-porarily out of work, and the provinces created a comprehensive social assistance program for people who were unable to work. But today, no social protections are available to individuals trapped in sporadic low-wage jobs and living in highly disad-vantaged urban neighbourhoods.

As a result, Canada's inner cities could end up in the down-ward spiral that American cities experienced in the postwar period. Many American cities have taken advantage of the past ten years of prosperity to make enormous investments to renew their inner cities and their infrastructure. Canadian cities have not been able to do this yet. But they must, if we are to preserve the quality of life for all. We need to make substantial investments in infrastructure and in opportunity for disadvantaged people to recover their self-reliance.

Time for Social Renewal

This is a big agenda. But the time has come to start thinking big. Clearly, Canada has to make some strategic choices. We need to balance the investments that will create more room to manoeuvre—paying down the debt—with the need for more public and private investment that gives citizens the tools they need to be successful in the competitive markets of the twenty-first century.

Canada's focus can now shift from economic survival to social and economic renewal. The policy challenge is to create a durable synergy where economic and social policies reinforce each other and jointly contribute to Canada's success. In that environment, all Canadians can believe they have a good chance of participating in that success.

(*For more detail on some of these ideas see* Toward a Common Citizenship: Canada's Social and Economic Choices, *at www.cprn.org.*)

Bob Rae

Bob Rae, *who served as premier of Ontario from 1990 to 1995, is a partner at Goodmans LLP,* where his clients include companies, trade unions, charitable and non-governmental organizations, and governments themselves. Mr. Rae is the national spokesperson of the Leukemia Research Fund; served as chief negotiator for the Canadian Red Cross Society in its restructuring; is a member of the Security and Intelligence Review Committee; and sits on numerous boards, including Tembec Inc., the University of Toronto, the Canadian Institute of Advanced Research, and the Royal Conservatory of Music. Mr. Rae was elected eight times to federal and provincial parliaments as a member of the NDP and has written two books, *From Protest to Power* and *The Three Questions*. He is a graduate of the University of Toronto, where he received his B.A. and law degree, and was a Rhodes Scholar, studying at Oxford University.

GOODMANS

GOODMANS LLP • BARRISTERS & SOLICITORS
TORONTO • VANCOUVER • HONG KONG

250 YONGE STREET
SUITE 2400
TORONTO, ONTARIO
CANADA M5B 2M6
TEL: 416.979.2211
FAX: 416.979.1234
www.goodmans.ca

M E M O R A N D U M

To: **The Prime Minister of Canada**

From: **Bob Rae** | *Former Premier of Ontario, and Partner, Goodmans LLP*

Subject: **Time for an Activist Agenda**

There will always be a temptation, with opponents on all sides of the spectrum in great disarray, to believe that sitting quietly should somehow be the order of the day.

That would be a great mistake. There is much to be done, because the condition of the people is still not what it needs to be. Too many are poor and badly housed; too many children are growing up without the chance to live to their greatest potential; too many frail and elderly are ending their days without access to the kind of care that would allow them to live in dignity.

The welfare state is not some kind of fortress that has simply to be protected from neo-conservative assault. The historic mission of liberalism has been to understand that market freedoms are an important advance on the alternatives, and yet that capitalism on its own produces much unfairness and much hardship. People want to live in an enterprise economy and at the same time want to live in a society that values their citizenship, their sense of participation, their individual humanity, and their commitment to the wider community.

Canada's commitment to improving the lives of its people is in constant need of attention and renewal. The appointment of Roy Romanow to look at health care shows an understanding that this most important achievement of the Canadian welfare state can't be taken for granted. While it is important to wait for his recommendations, the government even now should be preparing its response to three major challenges.

The first is that the cost of drugs is now out of sight for a great many Canadians, and access to good medicine has to include access to pharmaceutical treatment. Why could not the federal government see this as a national program, which while it could not be "free" at the beginning could certainly be tied to the tax system and the patient's ability to pay? Ontario's Trillium Plan, which focuses on the issue of catastrophic drug costs, is a first step—you could readily devise a Maple Leaf Plan for all Canadians.

The second issue is, of course, the care that must increasingly be provided to seniors and many others at home, rather than in an institutional setting. An aging population will very much need these services. Every province is doing something but we are not learning enough from each other. The federal government could become a more reliable financial partner as this part of the health care system steadily expands.

Finally, another key issue for the national government is helping to ensure that the governance and management of the health care system are less partisan, less political, and less subject to the whims of political change. There is a lot of evidence that Canadians value this system too much to see it constantly turned into a political football. Again there is much that the national government can do to encourage stable funding, more professional management, a greater capacity for innovation and change within the system itself, and more attention to long-term results. That is starting to happen, but more has to be done. There will always be much resistance, but it is clear that the status quo won't be enough.

Three Issues Demanding Federal Leadership

Three other issues are crying out for federal leadership. Many other advanced economies are ahead of us in housing and child care. We are doing less on housing across the country than we did thirty years ago. That makes no sense. There is strong evidence that the failure of both federal and provincial governments in social housing is producing a significant crisis in most of our urban centres. We can trace the reasons for the decline— but there can be no question that shelter has suffered dramatically as a result of cutbacks, and as a result we are at risk of facing a genuine disaster in the next five to ten years. This is not something the provinces can do on their own. That was the tough lesson that had to be learned in the 1930s, and again in the post-war era. All levels of government will have to work hard together lest we reap a whirlwind of homelessness for the next generation.

Child care has also been pretty much of an orphan, again largely because the provinces, with some notable exceptions, have failed to understand the implications of the social and economic changes that have transformed the nature of the modern family. A lack of attention to children in the earliest years has devastating consequences for the future of these children. We all end up paying for it with more problems in school, more conflicts with the law, more adolescents in trouble, more young men and women in jail, and more violence in the home. France, the Netherlands, and the Scandinavian countries all handle this challenge better than we do, and there is no reason we have to lag so far behind.

Both housing and child care should be showcases for the social union agreement. Federal financial surpluses should neither be an excuse for profligacy nor for false economies. Investments in housing and early childhood education across the country would more than pay for themselves, and their success will obviously require strong participation from the provinces. Every effort should be made to bring them to the table. Their fear will be that any new programs will be short-lived, and termination down the road would leave the provinces on the hook for significant new spending. The federal government will have to do more to show that it understands that no advanced economies have been able to move forward successfully without a commitment to proper housing for its people and early childhood education for its youngest citizens. These are not frills or fads. They are as important as health care.

Liberals should not be afraid of the tax question. The point is that taxes should be fair, government should be run efficiently, and there should be every effort to ensure the tax system provides the proper incentives. We could even sell higher taxes on energy consumption if they were combined with much more generous approaches to tax credits for people with lower incomes and bigger families. The Child Tax Credit and the other credits in the current *Income Tax Act* for people on lower incomes already provide you a sense of direction. Give these the deep improvements they need.

A more creative approach to energy and road pricing, combined with the tax relief, could also provide the opportunity for a renewed federal leadership in transportation, particularly urban transit. The quality of our urban life depends on this renewal and this investment.

Above all, avoid the twin mantras of ever-lowering taxes for the wealthy and ever-increasing taxes for most people. The right's fixation on cutting income taxes for upper income folks is a thinly veiled attempt to impoverish the ability of governments to respond to compelling public needs. The old left's insensitivity to the burden of ever-increasing taxes on the income of ordinary Canadians is a demonstration that they have fallen out of touch.

Finally, never forget the vulnerability of those who have been relegated to the margin of Canadian society. The key is to recognize that it is only access to education and work that will make a difference. This is where the effort must be focused. Passive income support that does not provide these opportunities is a dead end. There should be no illusion that a more activist approach will save money. In the near term, it will not. But when one considers the population explosion in Canada's native communities, for example, the alternative is a neglect that will foster truly disastrous consequences for the future. The engagement in working to build productive communities across the country is not one option. It is the only option.

This is not to say that self-government for Canada's Aboriginal people is unimportant. The old condescension has to end. But we have to put more meat on the constitutional bones.

Liberalism is not just about our individual freedom to do as we please, to make the money we want, to go our own way. All those things are inevitable features of living in the kind of market economy we do. But we also have to respond to the freedoms identified by Roosevelt and Churchill in the middle of the Atlantic when Canada was at war: freedom from want, from hunger and from fear, as well as from tyranny. Those values mean that the commitments to social democracy and liberalism can never be complacent. There is much work to be done.

Raisa Deber

Raisa Deber *is a professor of health policy in the Department of Health Policy, Management and Evaluation at the University of Toronto's faculty of medicine.* She has lectured and published extensively on Canadian health policy, and advised numerous local, provincial, national, and international bodies as well as serving on editorial boards and review panels. Her current research focuses on Canadian health policy. She is the director of a CIHR funded research alliance, M-THAC, an acronym for From Medicare to Home and Community: Overtaking the Limits of Publicly Funded Health Care in Canada. Projects include definitions of "medical necessity," public and private roles in the financing and delivery of health services, and the study of medical decision-making and issues surrounding patient empowerment.

Born in Toronto, she received her Ph.D. in political science from the Massachusetts Institute of Technology.

Department of Health Administration
Faculty of Medicine, University of Toronto

2nd Fl., McMurrich Bldg, 12 Queen's Park Cres. W.
Toronto, Ontario M5S 1A8
Fax: (416) 978-7350   Tel: (416)

M E M O R A N D U M

To: **The Prime Minister of Canada**

From: **Raisa Deber** | *Professor of Health Policy,*
University of Toronto

Subject: **Curing Health Care**

Health care is in crisis. That is nothing new; health care is always in crisis. Although medicare is on balance extraordinarily successful, since its inception provincial governments, doctors, nurses, and hospitals have always insisted that more money is needed. Yet the new money the federal government just put into the Canada Health and Social Transfer does not appear to have solved anything. If anything, the cries of crisis are louder. It is essential to move beyond the "blame game" to preserve and enhance a social program that is of primary importance to Canadians. There is no shortage of suggestions about what should be done; a plethora of fine reports have made reform suggestions. The purpose of this memo is to suggest what your government should do about it.

As you recognize, politically the federal government is in a difficult position in trying to manage medicare. Constitutionally, most of health care resides clearly within provincial jurisdiction, the consequence of a passing mention of "hospitals" when the Fathers of Confederation enumerated provincial responsibilities in the 1867 *British North America Act.* I do not need to remind you that many provincial governments—backed by the Official

Opposition—guard provincial jurisdiction carefully and will be highly resistant to perceived intrusions.

Their preferred option is for the federal government to continue to enhance provincial revenues and leave provincial governments free to set their own priorities. An aggressive federal intervention to sustain medicare by implementing overdue reforms will evoke strong reactions from those for whom principles of decentralized federalism outweigh health policy issues. Over the past decades, the trend within Canada has been to further decentralize policy authority; reversing that will not be simple.

Continuation of the "just-send-money" approach, however, has two significant weaknesses that, taken together, erode accountability for the funds so transferred and threaten the sustainability of medicare. The first weakness is legislative: Although everyone pledges allegiance to the famous five terms and conditions of the 1984 *Canada Health Act*—universality, comprehensiveness, portability, accessibility, and public administration—few appear to recognize the extent to which the act is shaped by the earlier legislation that it replaced. The 1957 *Hospital Insurance and Diagnostic Services Act* shared the costs of provincial hospital insurance plans; the 1966 *Medical Care Act* similarly cost-shared insurance for physician services. Their policy legacy is that the current act's definition of insured services is still written in terms of who delivers those services (physicians) or where they are delivered (hospitals). Although the act does not prohibit provincial governments from insuring other services, it does not require them to do so.

From 1957 to 2001: A Shift in Health Delivery

In 1957, however, when we started down this road, people who were ill were likely to be in a hospital. The *Canada Health Act* still ensures that most of those costs will be met by public financing. In 2001, however, technology has allowed more and more care to be delivered at home or in the community, and advances in pharmaceuticals and telecommunications are likely to accelerate that trend. In consequence, as the National Forum on Health pointed out, and as many subsequent studies and reports have reiterated, the comprehensiveness condition is in immediate need of updating. As technology allows care to shift from hospital to home and community, we are seeing what the Canadian Medical Association has termed "passive privatization."

All of those who must manage budgets recognize what has been called the First Law of Cost Containment: The easiest way to contain costs is to shift them to someone else. Accordingly, all stakeholders are busily engaged in cost shifting. Provincial governments are not immune from the incentive to reduce their own health care costs by shifting costs to third-party payers—including employers—and to individuals and their families, even though total costs and the burden on the Canadian economy may be higher. Despite the incentives for provinces to passively privatize, we must recognize that many provinces have resisted this trend in the interests of their residents, and do provide innovative and generous coverage for such services as home care, outpatient pharmaceuticals, rehabilitation, and mental health. However, there are no national standards, and both the cost of and access to such services can vary considerably, both across and within provinces. In consequence, Canada does indeed have two-tier medicine, but that is primarily found in the sectors moving outside of medicare such as home care, outpatient pharmaceuticals, and rehabilitation. Canada already has among the lowest proportions of public financing of all OECD countries, but the private payment tends to be concentrated in particular sectors (which have also seen the greatest cost escalation).

As is increasingly being recognized, poor coverage of community-based services can have perverse consequences; it can increase pressure on the more expensive publicly funded portions of the system. A person who cannot receive nursing care at home or who cannot afford needed medications is likely to turn up—far sicker—at a hospital emergency room. Some action to ensure cost control and availability of medically necessary services, regardless of where they are provided, is long overdue. However, it is less clear that all such services will fit well within the *Canada Health Act* framework; a companion bill may be more appropriate.

The second weakness is the clear failure of the 1977 federal experiment with block funding. In that year, Ottawa took three formerly cost-shared programs—hospital insurance, medical insurance, and postsecondary education—and transformed them into the Established Programs Financing (EPF). Although nominal figures are published on "federal health care transfers," in actuality those transfers merely became part of provincial general revenue. Indeed, about half of the transfer was given in the form of tax points, which moved these resources beyond federal policy control. Tax points would allow provincial governments to raise more revenue without affecting total tax burdens, if provincial tax increases moved in to the "tax room" vacated by the reduced federal rates. Worse, the efforts to restore fiscal stability in Ottawa led to a unilateral change in the indexing formula; this in turn meant that an ever-shrinking proportion of federal transfers were in the form of cash. In 1996, Ottawa compounded the problem by taking another cost-shared program—the Canada Assistance Plan—and combined it with EPF to form the new Canada Health and Social Transfer, while slashing federal payments. As the Auditor General has noted, we are also no longer able to identify federal health transfers. The transition to EPF after 1977 led to major and continuing cuts by provincial governments to postsecondary education (where no terms and conditions applied); the federal cuts to the Canada Health and Social Transfer were also reflected in provincial cuts to those welfare programs once cost-shared under the Canada Assistance Plan. One might even argue that health funding was not cut at all, but was preserved at the expense of those other important programs.

At any rate, provincial spending priorities have been within provincial control for almost a quarter of a century. In actuality, even the untargeted federal funds in the Canada Health and Social Transfer are important only as they affect provincial fiscal capacity. Nonetheless, Ottawa has lost the propaganda war. The federal-provincial funding arrangements are too arcane for easy sound bites. Provincial governments have successfully argued that they had to cut health care because they received too little money from the federal government; at the same time they were able to cut taxes and some even sent cheques to all of their citizens. From a health policy standpoint, future federal contributions should not be incorporated into the Canada Health and Social Transfer. However, your government will have to decide whether turning away from untargeted transfers for health care is worth the inevitable political battle.

Removing Partisanship

At this time, it is hard to recall that the critical legislation of 1957 and 1966 was passed with all-party approval. Medicare should not be a partisan issue. It has been demonstrated that we can obtain considerable cost efficiencies through a single payer for those services that we believe should be available universally, on the basis of need. Under those circumstances, it is foolish to argue that we require a mix of public and private financing because we "cannot afford" such services from the public purse. If society cannot afford universal care from a single payer, it cannot afford it at the higher prices paid within the mix of public and private payment. Attempts to shift costs away from government will only reduce the economic competitiveness of business if private insurance costs are placed on payrolls, or burden individuals and their families, and lead to preventable mortality and morbidity if they are not.

Despite rhetoric to the contrary, the only rigidity provided by the *Canada Health Act* is its requirement that all Canadian residents be insured for all medically necessary physician and hospital services. Canada does not need the "flexibility" to de-insure sick people, or increase total costs (and reduce equity) by imposing user fees for necessary physician and hospital services. Provinces are free to introduce whatever other experiments they wish. The barriers have been political—in particular, dealing with powerful interest groups and public resistance to changes that they (with some cause) fear will increase costs and reduce access.

This insistence that the problems do not arise from the current reliance upon public financing for certain services, or the constraints of the *Canada Health Act*, does not mean that there are not real problems that must be dealt with. One pressing problem is determining the boundaries between public and private; not all health care services are medically necessary, and it follows that not all need be paid for publicly. Determining the boundaries, however, will not be simple. Another pressing problem is health human resources—how much are we willing to pay health care workers, and will good people be willing to work for the agreed upon wages and working conditions? In the short term, we have achieved considerable cost savings by capping physician incomes, using less skilled (and less costly) labour, and forcing many nurses into part-time or casual work. In the long run, many of these measures have been "penny wise and pound foolish" and are unlikely to be sustainable. A third problem is ensuring that services are appropriate and of high quality—long waiting lists for necessary care are categorically unacceptable (and usually cost-inefficient as well).

However, few of those policy issues are within the ambit of the federal government. Indeed, few are even controlled by provincial governments. It must be recognized that although 70% of Canadian health costs come from public sources, virtually all of those who deliver health services are private (albeit often not-for-profit) individuals and organizations. As such, payers have remarkably few policy levers to control what services are delivered, their appropriateness, or their quality. Structural reforms to achieve such levers—such as primary care reform—will also be contentious.

On one level, the critics are right. More resources may indeed be needed. No one can function at peak efficiency all of the time; burnout results. Hospitals cannot continue to operate at 95% occupancy. Doctors and nurses cannot be expected to work with minimal support. There are always ways of increasing efficiency; simply squeezing those working in the system, however, has reached the point of diminishing returns.

In this era of complaint and grievance, it may sound idealistic to call for partnership and cooperation. Yet medicare is a clear example where most of those involved have common goals. We all wish for a sustainable, efficient, high-quality system with motivated and skilled workers, albeit at an affordable cost. Fortunately, health care workers go into their professions because of a genuine desire to help others. Patients continue to trust doctors and nurses. Business recognizes that it will benefit from maintaining medicare. Rather than burdening payrolls, it is past time for political parties and all levels of government to transcend their perennial bickering and work with providers and the public to stop the blame game and get on with it.

Steven Lewis

Steven Lewis *is a health policy and research consultant based in Saskatoon, and adjunct professor of health policy at the University of Calgary.* Prior to resuming a full-time consulting practice, he spent seven years as CEO of the Health Services Utilization and Research Commission in Saskatchewan. He was a member of the National Forum on Health; the Federal-Provincial Advisory Committee on Health Services; the boards of directors of the Canadian Nurses' Association and the Saskatchewan Health Information Network; and the Council of the Canadian Population Health Initiative. Currently he sits on the governing council of the Canadian Institutes of Health Research.

ACCESS CONSULTING LTD.

STEVEN LEWIS
PRESIDENT

211 – 4th Avenue South
Saskatoon, SK (CANADA) S7K 1N1
Telephone (306) 343-1007
Facsimile (306) 343-1071
E0mail sj.lewis@home.com

M E M O R A N D U M

To: **The Prime Minister of Canada**

From: **Steven Lewis** | *Consultant on Health Policy,*
Access Consulting Ltd.

Subject: **How a Focus on Quality—Not Cheques—
Will Improve Medicare**

For a decade, public opinion polls have chronicled Canadians' waning confidence in the ability of governments to deliver the medicare goods. Yet once inside the door of the system, Canadians are very pleased with the quality of services they receive. Unfortunately, their confidence is misplaced. Quality is the number one problem in health care in our country —not money, not bureaucracy, not technology. And the failure to focus on it is why every major attempt to fix medicare has failed.

Indeed, a strange indifference marks our response to the abundant evidence of quality problems. Take drugs. They are routinely overprescribed, resulting in many avoidable admissions to hospital, particularly among the elderly. Often, appropriately prescribed drugs are useless when patients do not take them as indicated: For example, a Saskatchewan study found that only a quarter of people stayed on their cholesterol-lowering medications long enough to benefit. As well, expensive drugs that are no better than their cheaper counterparts are thoughtlessly prescribed and consumed, wasting tens of millions of dollars as quality is ignored.

Human memory cannot possibly keep straight the indications and contraindications for the 20,000 or so drugs on the market or remember which pairs are far apart in price but equivalent in therapeutic value. Sanely, experts have developed software to aid decisions and reduce prescribing error; insanely, most physicians don't use them. Pharmacists know far more about drugs but tradition and legislation reduce many of them to the status of passive pill-counters. Adoption of sensible redesign is slow; the result is waste, harm, and risk.

We have, free of charge on the World Wide Web, an ominous wake-up call from the U.S. Institute of Medicine. Its landmark report last year on clinical error estimates that as many as 100,000 Americans are killed annually by avoidable therapeutic or diagnostic errors. The United States pursues quality improvement far more vigorously than Canada and it would be hard to imagine that our error rates are lower. We can plausibly estimate that 5,000 to 10,000 Canadians—or more—are killed each year by our failure to implement systems to eliminate error. That's 15 to 30 people every day—more than die of breast cancer or traffic accidents.

Waiting Lists in Perspective

A national preoccupation is waiting lists, whether for cancer therapy in Ontario or hip replacement surgery across the country. And wait we do: A quarter of Ontarians report difficulties obtaining front-line medical care; 13,000 people awaited elective surgery in Saskatoon in February 2001; it can take months to see a neurologist in many cities; non-urgent MRI scans can take six months or more. The fact that Canada has about as many MRI machines per capita as Poland and the Czech Republic has apparently become such a symbolic humiliation that it scars the fragile Canadian psyche. (That no one documented the impact of this ostensible shortage prior to the rush to install new machines is curiously overlooked.)

At regular intervals, doctors, interest groups, the media, and politicians declare a state of emergency and call for action. The action of choice is the writing of cheques. Lineups temporarily shorten, but within months the problems recur. Directions for a failed solution to waiting lists: Add money. Add capacity. Repeat.

Interestingly, where we have data, it appears that the dimensions of the problem are vastly overstated—average wait times hardly changed at all during the 1990s despite financial constraint while the system increased volumes. But let's go with perception. If so many believe there is a serious and chronic waiting problem, one would think that the management of waiting lists would therefore be a top priority.

And for some kinds of life-threatening conditions—cancer and heart disease—some jurisdictions have developed standardized assessments of need, acceptable wait times, and well-ordered queues. But for elective procedures, there is virtually no management at all. Wait lists are kept in individual physicians' offices—the doctors, therefore, "own" their lists. The health regions established in nine provinces to integrate services, distribute resources fairly, and attend to the health of their populations would, in a quality-oriented system, manage and oversee waiting lists in a fair, rational, and transparent manner. But they rarely have consolidated, up-to-date wait list information. They do not know the condition of people on wait lists and do not track whether and how waiting affects quality of life or outcomes.

There are no standards or directions: Different physicians have different thresholds for putting people on waiting lists, which guarantees inequitable access unless someone is minding the store to even the playing field. The "management" method of choice for the waiting lists is chronological—first on, first off the list, irrespective of the severity of need. Often very long lists persist alongside very high rates of service. Supply induces demand that induces supply. We watch, and we shrug.

These realities are scandalous and as yet uncorrected. International literature reveals that management, not money, will solve waiting list problems. A large U.S. health care organization reduced its wait times for routine consultations from two months to one day with no additional money or staff simply by paying attention to peaks and valleys in demand and scheduling effectively. New Zealand has a nation-wide system for managing wait lists. That's organization, that's problem solving, and that's quality.

Why don't Canadians focus on quality? One reason is what amounts to a transnational paradox. The American political culture values freedom, choice, and individual rights. Canada has a more collectivist and balanced tradition. But in health care, the reverse is true: Clinical autonomy and the right to practise unevaluated, unaccountably, and unmanaged is almost sacred in this country, while south of the border, the ethos is measure, report, and improve (to be sure, in the context of a grotesquely expensive and uneven system). The sixth principle of medicare is: don't ask, don't tell. Especially don't tell the public.

Another cause of the quality problem is underinvestment in the tools essential to improvement. We spend less than 2% of the health care budget on information technology. Nonprofit leaders in health care in the United States spend up to 8% or more. We do not have a real-time electronic health record accessible to any provider, anywhere, on a need-to-know basis. So we repeat tests; doctors and nurses often lack information crucial to diagnosis and care; and the potential for error abounds.

Health care is probably the most information-intensive industry in the world, where the science can change weekly. Yet most organizations are crippled by clumsy and fragmented information systems that cannot easily talk to each other. Under those circumstances, effective and efficient resource use is an impossibility.

It is time to rethink what the root problems are and redesign the system to extract quality from the $95 billion we spend on health care. Every moment of delay will compound the harm and the waste. The grace period for the system is rapidly shrinking in the face of highly publicized tragedies and the growing recognition among the media that quality and error are stories with legs. The blood supply fiasco and the paediatric cardiology deaths in Winnipeg are but the tip of the iceberg, just as the first revelations of residential school abuse led to a wave of further cases and possibly billions of dollars in restitution. As the public and the media come to realize that error is not occasional and random, but the inevitable consequence of faulty system design, the fallout will be widespread. The still-high degree of public confidence in the quality of services received will erode. And where error and skepticism abound, litigation follows.

Ottawa's Role: A Commitment to Quality

What can Ottawa do? First, it can highlight and lead a commitment to quality. The federal government ceded its moral authority to guide medicare in the 1990s, when it unilaterally reduced its transfer payments to the provinces as part of the effort to get its fiscal house in order. It has bought itself some credibility with the September 2000 Accord that promises $23.5 billion over five years, a 7% boost to the public system. But it can no longer mandate new programs or hold itself out as the custodian of medicare—at least not for the foreseeable future.

It can, however, provide intellectual leadership and use money to lever a change in perspective. A billion of the new federal dollars is contingent on the provinces agreeing to report on how well the system is performing. That condition has groundbreaking potential but it remains far from certain that truly rigorous, timely, and standardized reports will result. Ottawa should press to make it happen.

Ottawa should also sponsor some concrete initiatives to boost quality. Among them are the following:

- Create a National Quality Council with a mandate to develop performance indicators and quality improvement tools; launch a sustained error-reduction initiative; and report publicly on performance.

- Fund and champion a standardized national approach to electronic health records—the core of the information system essential to high-quality care, the key to the efficient use of resources, and the building block of first-class health services research.

- Sponsor major initiatives in curriculum development, accreditation, and certification of professionals that adapt the quality and teamwork ethos of other industries to health care.

- Influence federal granting agencies to fund research and training in quality improvement and error reduction.

Those are only examples of measures to advance nothing short of a cultural transformation in health care. If it is achieved, important dividends will accrue.

The first will flow from the fact that quality is cheaper than error. Dr. Donald Berwick, long at the leading edge of quality improvement in the United States, estimates potential savings of 30% by redesigning systems to eliminate error, waste, duplication, and inconvenience. Brigham and Women's Hospital in Boston estimated it saved $5 to $10 million simply by persuading doctors to replace often illegibly handwritten drug prescriptions with computerized prescription entry. Error rates fell, and nurses and clerks no longer had to spend hours deciphering hieroglyphs or chasing down doctors to confirm what they meant.

The second payoff is improved workforce morale. Doubtless health care workers are working harder and enjoying it less. They mistakenly believe money will solve the problem, as do governments. No industry with masses of disgruntled workers will produce quality products. A quality orientation will make the workplace saner, produce better results, eliminate useless work, and effect a shift from working harder to working smarter.

The third dividend is better health. A quality system prevents problems rather than fixing them when they have become serious. Intervening upstream costs a lot less than rescuing downstream. Fewer errors mean fewer adverse events and reduced waste. A hallmark of quality is standardization: doing the same thing in the same circumstances. That should result in the disappearance of often-huge variations in the rates of surgery and diagnostic procedures that are so common today. Standardization also increases equity because all citizens are far more likely to get the same treatment for the same problem in an equally timely fashion.

Mr. Prime Minister, leading the quality revolution requires tact and commitment. You will soon see your $23.5 billion disappearing into the insatiable maw of health care—much of it directly into the pockets of the doctors and nurses who have seen the cash and have begun negotiating for all of it ($40,000 a year extra per doctor and 22% more over two years per nurse in Alberta commandeered early in 2001, with other provinces sure to follow). For a few dollars more you can actually create change instead of retarding it by propping up the status quo. That will be leadership, and a true legacy. Canadians (though not the provinces) want Ottawa involved in health care; the key is picking your spots. Quality is spot one.

Peter Holle

Peter Holle *is president of the Frontier Centre for Public Policy*, a regional think tank based in Winnipeg that focuses on eastern prairie issues. The Frontier Centre conducts public policy research and education activities in several areas, including performance-based government, social policy renewal, and the new economy. Mr. Holle, a management consultant with a background in public sector reform, was a senior policy analyst for the province of Saskatchewan in the 1980s, where he worked on regulatory reform and the privatization of government services and assets. He has a Master's of Business Administration from the University of Wisconsin at Madison.

FRONTIER CENTRE

FOR PUBLIC POLICY

PETER HOLLE
President

201-63 Albert Street
Winnipeg, Manitoba
Canada • R3B 1G4
Phone: (204) 957-1567
Fax: (204) 957-1570
E-mail:
newideas@fcpp.org

M E M O R A N D U M

To: **The Prime Minister of Canada**

From: **Peter Holle** | *President,*
Frontier Centre for Public Policy

Subject: **Universal Medical Savings Accounts**

Canada's medicare system is progressively deteriorating. It faces recurrent crises in its present form despite a continuous, decades-long allocation of more tax resources. At the same time, Canadians clearly want to ensure guaranteed, universal access to medical services. A new medicare model has the potential to retain universality, restore service levels, control costs, and introduce transparency and accountability to the system. That model, Universal Medical Savings Accounts (UMSAs), allocates existing public funding directly to individual citizen-consumers of health care services.

Currently, federal and provincial governments underwrite medicare budgets through a complex system of block grants to medical authorities. With UMSAs, the same money would be divided among individual health care consumers, each of whom would receive it in the form of credits deposited to a dedicated health care account. With the exception of a mandatory requirement to purchase insurance coverage for long-term and catastrophic care, spending from the account would be controlled by the account holder. Hospitals, clinics, and doctors would charge patients for services rendered, with payments made from individual accounts. Any money left in the account would remain the property of the account-holder.

Here's how the system would work:

- At the beginning of each fiscal year, health authorities would deposit each citizen's share of the medicare budget into a dedicated bank account in that person's name. Based on recent expenditures, a family of four in Manitoba or Saskatchewan, for example, would receive between $6,000 and $7,000. Each account holder would gain access to those funds through an electronic debit card.

- Withdrawals from the account would be allowed only to pay for health care services.

- Minor, non-catastrophic events requiring a visit to a clinic or doctor would be paid by direct electronic debit from an individual's or family's account.

- Individuals would cover themselves against catastrophic events by purchasing insurance from competing companies.

- Money not spent would be rolled over and left to accumulate tax-free over the account holder's lifetime until the fund reached some predetermined amount sufficient to create an income stream that would cover future medical emergencies (perhaps $200,000).

- The funds would belong to the consumer and his or her estate.

- The special cases that arise—the small minority who run out of funds or have special needs—would be accommodated separately with extra government assistance.

Advantages of the System

UMSAs perform well according to the following three common criteria of high-performance public policy: transparency, neutrality, and separation.

1. TRANSPARENCY

UMSAs offer a public health care commitment visible to all. Currently, few people understand how much the government spends on health care per family. Under an UMSA system, public spending becomes highly visible to all.

Consumers are rewarded under the system for not overusing services. Individuals benefit personally because they keep funds not spent on unnecessary use of health care resources. Society benefits from a more efficient use of capital, which frees it up for use elsewhere. Prices provide valuable information on costs and benefits, thereby enabling providers and consumers to make rational decisions without political involvement.

2. NEUTRALITY

Under this system, universality is preserved, as universal publicly funded access remains in place. The government still funds health care but no longer directly provides it. There is no bias toward a particular process—the system is neutral.

Incentives for efficiency are introduced. A decentralized, customer-sensitive system that reflects the decisions of millions of consumers replaces a less flexible single-provider monopoly. Competition creates pressure to contain costs, increase quality, and offer timely service. Consumers now drive what the system produces.

New technology is encouraged. The freedom to shop weeds out services and facilities that fail to please consumers, who vote with their UMSA funds by patronizing those that do. UMSA debit cards facilitate automated billing through low transaction costs. This reduces administrative overheads while providing customers with useful information on their health care purchases.

3. SEPARATION

The system separates politicians from operations. The task of elected officials is simplified. Resources are no longer allocated politically through a centrally planned system that has too little information to accommodate the complete range of individual health care needs and desires.

Elected officials withdraw from haphazard involvement in the operation and design of the delivery system. Separating public financing from private production allows the emergence of a framework within which flexibility in process and delivery methods maximizes outcomes.

Capital is released for public endowment. Government ownership is no longer required in a decentralized, competitive system in which the public financing function has been separated from production decisions. Billions of dollars in hospital assets can be transferred to charitable organizations or sold to doctor groups or insurance companies. The proceeds endow a public fund that helps low-income groups and special hardship cases purchase health care services. Lower taxes and a higher living standard follow this release of capital.

Creating Positive Incentives for Better Health Care

UMSAs not only motivate consumers to use the health care system intelligently by letting them keep the money they haven't spent, but they also reward providers for delivering services efficiently and effectively. Providers would design insurance plans to encourage healthier lifestyle choices (such as discounts for non-smokers) that would ultimately lower costs. UMSAs, if permitted a degree of flexibility, offer policy makers another lever to encourage better community-wide outcomes. For example, items such as exercise-club memberships might be paid through an individual's UMSA account.

Will a Consumer-Controlled System Work?

Medical Savings Accounts have proven successful in the few instances where they have been tried. Several American corporations offer coverage to their employees through their own private accounts. Hundreds of employee groups have enjoyed cost savings that range from 12% to 40%. Individual control over resources has produced high levels of personal satisfaction.

Singapore introduced a system of medical savings accounts in three stages, starting in 1984. Since then, the city-state has reduced its national spending on health care to a third of Canada's rate. Yet facilities are state-of-the-art, service is quick, and standards are high. Singapore boasts a life expectancy of seventy-seven years and a thriving economy.

Important Questions and Answers

Q: *Wouldn't the Universal Medical Saving Accounts system mean the privatization of medicare?*

A: Since the model maintains public funding at present levels, there is no change in the tax-funded public commitment to health care. The model will not function without giving consumers the ability to choose between competing providers. To achieve that, the government would transfer or sell the facilities it owns to interested parties, including health care professionals, doctor groups, insurance companies, and charitable organizations. While funding remains public, the production of health services would, in this practical sense, be necessarily privatized.

Q: *What about people who overspend their accounts before the year is up and are left with nothing in the account?*

A: They tend not to. Since account holders keep whatever they don't spend, they have a powerful incentive to husband the resource carefully. A special policy can be designed for the small minority who "fall through the cracks." Those costs would be covered by an endowment fund formed from the sale of facilities that would be part of the government's complete or partial relinquishing of direct monopoly ownership.

Q: *What happens to the money that accumulates in the account when an individual dies?*

A: Since the funds do not belong to the government, but to the individual consumer, they would remain the property of that person's estate. They would be passed on to the heirs of that estate, likely their children.

Q: *Will any accumulated funds not spent on health care services earn interest in the name of the consumer?*

A: The UMSA system would be like an RRSP where companies compete with different financial products to maximize the returns to individual account holders.

Q: *Wouldn't the return of individual billing create more administrative overhead?*

A: That may have been the case in the past, but electronic debit cards and technology are rapidly driving down transaction costs. A shift to an UMSA system would take advantage of this development. Even if changing the single-payer system resulted in slightly higher transaction costs, the savings in consumption and from increased efficiency in the use of resources would more than compensate for them.

Q: *One argument in favour of the single-provider model is that it saves unnecessary spending on billing administration. Won't a publicly funded competing-supplier system just waste money?*

A: That ignores the role accounting systems play in providing valuable information about production costs. Before it collapsed, the centrally planned Soviet economy "saved money" by neglecting to bother with accounting systems that tracked costs. Prices and costs provide the information that guides decisions in a competitive environment. Without them, no supplier can make rational pricing decisions.

Q: *Isn't health care too important to allow the profit motive in hospitals and clinics?*

A: Many groups have an ideological problem with the concept of profits. Lacking any sophisticated understanding of how markets work, they fail to understand that profits provide information that signals to the marketplace what services consumers are seeking. They automatically direct the use of resources toward the desired activities and services. High profits in particular markets will attract new entrants, expanding supply and reducing prices. Low profits and losses signal the opposite. Facilities that garner higher profits than others will do so because they offer more timely service of a higher quality. That creates a powerful incentive for providers to do their best.

Q: *Wouldn't insurance companies try to gouge consumers for long-term and catastrophic coverage?*

A: The best policy would be to maximize competition by not restricting or encumbering entry into the health care market. Competition among multiple providers in a market worth billions of dollars would prevent price gouging. To allay this concern, the government could allow each citizen a choice: Do you want to have a medical savings account that belongs to you, or do you want to remain in the current system? American companies that have allowed employees to stay with their existing managed-care plans or to use medical savings accounts have found that, within a short time, large majorities opt for the latter.

Q: *How much would comprehensive insurance coverage for extraordinary medical expenses cost?*

A: It would depend on the age of the account holder and the size of the deductible. The accompanying chart shows one estimate of the cost, calculated by using recent rates for equivalent insurance now available in the United States, assuming a $1,000 deductible. In each case, the size of the premiums leaves more than enough in the medical accounts to cover the cost of deductibles and out-of-pocket payments for minor health expenses.

Estimated Cost of Catastrophic Insurance Coverage

Demographic Status	Insurance Premium*	MSA Resources**	Balance
Single male, aged 25	$ 298	$1,750	$1,452
Single female, aged 25	633	1,750	1,117
Male and female, aged 35, with two children	$1,825	3,500	1,675
Male and female, aged 55	1,537	3,500	1,963

Adapted from *Healthy Incentives: Canadian Health Reform in an International Context,* edited by William McArthur, M.D., Cynthia Ramsay, and Michael Walker, with permission of The Fraser Institute.

* Insurance premiums from *Healthy Incentives: Canadian Health Reform in an International Context,* Fraser Centre, 1996.
** Based on $1,750 per person per year or $7,000 per family of four.

Q: *How do you prevent insurance companies from cherry-picking low-risk customers?*

A: You make it a condition of participating in the huge new market that they have to accept all applicants. The resultant higher level of risk would require slightly higher rates, which would socialize the expense of covering higher-cost patients over the entire market.

Q: *Would UMSA holders have to restrict their spending to gov-ernment-approved facilities and methods?*

A: The best policy would allow as much latitude as possible. A wide body of evidence supports the value of many therapies now regarded as "alternative medicine." Consumer choice— millions of people judging their worth instead of a few regula-tors—allows the market to determine their effectiveness. That promotes much greater innovation in solving health problems.

The government would have to set minimum quality-control standards, as it does in many other industries. It would have the power to delist any providers who failed to meet its criteria, making them ineligible for UMSA dollars.

Q: *What would happen to waiting lists?*

A: They would disappear. Waiting lists appear when the demand for services exceeds the supply in a system without prices. Since resources are not unlimited, the excess demand translates into shortages and lineups. In an UMSA system consumers control the money formerly spent by government on them. They would purchase services in line with their needs and desires. Providers would price their services to best attract customers. As in any normal market, prices would rise as demand increased. That would attract new suppliers. Supply would expand and prices would adjust downwards. The price mechanism furnishes us the signals we need to balance supply with demand—the dynamic that is missing in our present single-provider system.

Q: *Wouldn't UMSAs create a two-tier system in which wealthier people could ensure better service by paying more?*

A: We have a two-tier system now, one in which only those with deep pockets can seek care outside the country. People with fewer resources have no choice but to rely on the service offered by a single provider. UMSAs would expand their choices by allowing them to spend their resources wherever they wished.

Dr. Nancy Olivieri

Dr. Nancy Olivieri *is a professor of pediatrics and medicine at the University of Toronto.* The author of over 150 peer-reviewed papers, book chapters, and reviews, she focuses her current research efforts on the development of new therapies for patients with sickle cell disease and thalassemia in collaboration with scientists in Europe, Asia, the United States, and Canada. Dr. Olivieri remains on active staff at Toronto's Hospital for Sick Children and the Toronto General Hospital, where she cares for children and adults with blood diseases. She received her undergraduate degree in biology at the University of Toronto, her Doctor of Medicine at McMaster University in 1978, and did postgraduate training at McMaster, University of Toronto, and Harvard University. She is the recipient of the First Annual Whistleblower Award, British Columbia Freedom of Information and Privacy Association; the 1999 Ontario Ethics in Action Award; the Joe A. Callaway Award for Civic Courage, Shadeek Nader Foundation; and the Community Champion Award, Civil Justice Foundation.

SOCIAL
CANADA

Department of Medicine
Faculty of Medicine, University of Toronto
1 King's College Circle
Toronto, Ontario M5S 1A8
Fax: (416) 978-7230

MEMORANDUM

To: **The Prime Minister of Canada**

From: **Dr. Nancy Olivieri** | *Professor of Pediatrics and Medicine, University of Toronto*

Subject: **The Commercialization of Canadian University Research**

Over fifty years ago, Professor Harold Innis observed that "to buy universities is to destroy them, and with them, the civilization for which they stand." Since then more Canadians have recognized the pressures that the private sector is exerting, with escalating success, on individuals and institutions mandated to act in the public interest. My particular interest arises from personal experience with the consequences of the increasing control by Canada's largest and wealthiest private generic drug company over two clinical trials, both conducted at a publicly funded institution and supported by public money. But the story is much broader than my unhappy—far from unique, and regrettably ongoing—experience with Apotex Inc. and the University of Toronto.

The increasing commercialization of university research has major consequences that are ultimately destructive to the mission of a university. The university must serve the public interest—and no other. It must uphold academic freedom and scientific integrity; it must support the challenge—not the preservation—of the status quo. It must sustain and protect the unqualified pursuit and public dissemination of knowledge and truth. Those are not merely abstract moral principles. We have seen that public interest dims as a consideration for some university presidents and deans of medicine once they are presented with industry offers that they cannot, apparently, refuse. And we will see again, in clinical drug trials, that when those in authority do not resist such pressures, the protection of patients may be the first casualty.

As Professor Innis's warning illustrates, pressures to commercialize university research in Canada are not new. More recent, however, is the widespread endorsement of such pressures from Canada's government-sponsored committees. A 1988 Science Council of Canada report, the product of a three-year investigation of university-industry linkages, urged the reorientation of university activities to provide teaching and research *required* by the private sector, and that transfer of knowledge and technology to the private sector be recognized in the hiring of professors and rewarded through their academic promotion. Canadian universities were warned that they had little choice: If universities did not reach out to meet *the needs of society* [emphasis added], "these needs will be satisfied elsewhere." (Note that in these debates it is not uncommon for industry interests to become the needs of society.)

A decade later, the 1999 Report of the Expert Panel on the Commercialization of University Research written at the behest of the Prime Minister's Advisory Council on Science and Technology echoed the exhortation that Canadian universities "redefine" their missions. The panel also urged that the country's universities add to their three traditional roles of teaching, research, and community service a fourth endeavour, innovation, which was defined as "the process of bringing new goods and services to market." Since the panel included six corporate industry representatives and two university administrators, without any expert engaged in the type of research under discussion or a single representative from the social sciences or humanities, that recommendation shouldn't surprise Canadians—but it *should* alarm us.

What's wrong with the increasing corporate domination of university research?

Briefly, the ideals of academic science are that it be conducted openly and be freely exchanged and disseminated after peer review. Academic science is often long-range, curiosity-driven, and apparently impractical. By contrast, corporate science is directed, secretive, and economically driven.

How does the trend toward this form of research conducted in university settings affect Canadians? I'll limit myself here to six concerns, although there are many more:

- First, the commercialization of university research directs the research *questions*: what is studied and who studies it. As we fall more under the spell of corporate research, who will fund areas of study in the social sciences and the humanities that are not immediately (or possibly, never) commercially exploitable? Who will fund research in treatments of diseases in emerging countries where exploitable markets do not exist?

- Second, the commercialization of university research directs the research *answers*: what is (and is not) made public. If the scientific findings threaten companies' commercial interests they are often suppressed, and parallel attempts made to discredit their source, the investigator. Examples abound in which universities financially beholden to the sponsoring company have outdone interested corporations in vilifying such investigators. In 1999, the president of the University of Toronto, whose professors took a public stand which threatened the commercial interests of Apotex, later petitioned the prime minister to relax federal restrictions against Apotex, the promised donor of university largesse. Even if other university leaders do not emulate this grievous example, many investigators may distort the *finding* to the *funding*. Dozens of studies now indicate that drugs may be reported as effective, or ineffective, according to whether the company is paying a researcher to provide the opinion.

- Third, the commercialization of university research decides who *asks* and *answers* the questions in this, and in the next, generation of scientists. If the philosophy of the Science

Council of Canada or the Expert Panel is embraced, industry-friendly researchers following a corporate agenda will be hired and rewarded by promotion at Canadian universities. As well, the matching of public funding to private funding is pervasive in several prominent granting programs. Professors conducting research without commercial interests are rarely funded through these programs.

- Fourth, the commercialization of university research benefits the interests of private corporations at the expense of those of public citizens. The private sector can use universities and academic hospitals to privatize its profits and socialize its losses. For a small investment, companies gain access to research establishments that remain, in Canada, largely supported by public money. Companies use the resources of medical schools—the people, their training and expertise, the laboratories, the collaborations already in existence—for a relatively minor investment. In clinical drug trials, for example, the costs of tests required by the trial protocol may be supported covertly by provincial health plans at no expense to companies developing the drug. The costs of labour in clinical hospital laboratories and the support of secretaries and lab technologists who may carry out some percentage of their duties in the course of the clinical trial are often provided to these companies, courtesy of the public sector.

- Fifth, the commercialization of university research threatens public health. Canada's Health Protection Branch has become an agency highly influenced by pressure from drug companies to license inadequately studied drugs.

- Finally, the commercialization of university research threatens public trust. Alone in our society, the university stands for truth—for a place where dissent is rewarded and raw power is tempered. It is supposed to be a place where areas of study *not* for sale are examined—a place where the scientist may pursue knowledge for the common good while holding to the highest ideals of scientific integrity. The reaction of Canadians to the Apotex/University of Toronto scandal shows they want research that they can trust.

There may be difficulties with—and there will certainly be objections to—my recommended solutions. But if implemented as public policy, some of them might slow the race to the ethical bottom that some have succumbed to:

- First, increase *truly public* funding—over and above public funding that depends on matching from industry partners—to the national granting agencies. Canadians are willing to be taxed for the sake of unbiased science. The Canadian Foundation for Innovation, the strategic grants program, the matching grants programs, and the 21st Century Chair program provide increased opportunities for some forms of research. At the same time, we all need to recognize that these programs also represent opportunities for private corporations to steer the direction of publicly funded research. Those programs, therefore, should not replace true "no-strings attached," curiosity-driven research that industry is not interested in funding. For every dollar directed into the above initiatives, the Canadian government should provide a dollar toward programs that do not demand that the research answers possess potential commercial value.

- Second, prohibit researchers receiving stock or equity interest, consulting fees and honoraria, industry-sponsored trips, meals or other benefits, and any decision-making position in a company that may appear to be affected by the results of their work. Following the conclusion of the trial, those prohibitions should remain in place for a period of three years. Government officials are not allowed to participate in any matter in which they have a financial conflict of interest—and university professors and physicians should be held to the same standard. That would of course not eliminate the influence of financial conflicts of interest with the company sponsoring the research but it could reduce them.

- Third, within the federal granting programs, limit the financial and administrative ties between corporations and the investigator or institution in any research supported by industry. Practically, that would mean annual industry funding to university investigators over and above the full costs of a study would be restricted. (Such funding often, in essence, is provided by companies as a reward for time and expertise.) Whether the researcher participated in one or several industry-supported trials, he or she should be restricted to $10,000 over the costs of the studies per academic year. Any monies over and above this amount would be forwarded to the university, to be administered by a new method described below.

- Fourth, to prevent public funding of private profit, demand that drug companies assume full and often hidden costs of clinical trials conducted in academic settings. The expenses that should be placed squarely at the door of corporations include the costs of support staff that may carry out some percentage of their daily or weekly duties for the company's study.

- Fifth, insist that universities distribute "overhead" or other money derived from industry funding evenly to the university community, to restore the balance of funding toward other faculties, including the humanities. An academic institution customarily charges overhead to a company as a proportion of the total amount of a clinical trial or study. It is often exploited by university administrators to express favour toward academic staff who draw money from industry—increased salaries being one of the forms of approbation—and naturally fewer or no rewards are provided to those with less easy access to industry funding. That tilts the power to industry.

One way of restoring the balance within the system would be to place the money in a fund that is not accessible to and cannot be administered by either the investigator or dean. Ideally, the money within a university system could be administered by an independent panel that included representatives from nonprofit organizations, the governing council of the university, the faculties of both science and humanities, a disinterested industry representative, and members of other academic centres. The membership of this body could be revised on a regular basis. Funding administered through this panel would be awarded on a competitive basis to applicants from all university faculties, so not just those drawing corporate research monies benefit.

- Sixth, mandate the independence of public funders from their corporate partners in all decision making with respect to studies, including the publication of research results. An independent study panel whose members' identity would not be provided to the industry partner could review any proposed decisions. In my experience—and that of other investigators—the public may not be represented adequately currently by our public granting agencies. They have previously failed to resist, or protest, scientifically unjustified decisions by industry partners.

- Seventh, introduce policy mandating that Canadian universities realize a percentage return on any commercialization of a drug or technology developed within a university setting. Such monies would then be channelled to the publicly funded granting agencies.

- Eighth, don't make the protection of patients in clinical trials the responsibility of the lone investigator, who will always lack the resources to battle irresponsible corporate influence. Currently, the federal government's Health Protection Branch is dangerously deregulated. Decisions taken by the branch, driven by the private sector, have already exposed the public to harm. Under the current system, it is no longer necessary to show that a drug is effective to market it in Canada. Policy changes allow companies to sell first and do research later. That means thousands of Canadians will take drugs that may harm them. The mission of the Health Protection Branch is not to be sensitive to the interests of the pharmaceutical companies.

Like yours, Prime Minister, it is to serve the public interest.

Margaret Hillyard Little

Margaret Hillyard Little | *is an anti-poverty activist and academic who works in the area of single mothers on welfare, welfare and workfare reform, and retraining for women on welfare. She is jointly appointed to women's studies and political studies at Queen's University.* She is the author of *No Car, No Radio, No Liquor Permit: The Moral Regulation of Single Mothers in Ontario, 1920-1997*, which won the 1998 Chalmers Book Award, and is currently writing a book about an innovative retraining program in Regina that trains low-income women to be licensed carpenters. She is a recipient of the Chancellor's Research Award, which will allow her over a five-year period to study the impact of welfare reforms in Canada, the U.S., and Great Britian.

Institute of Women's Studies

Mackintosh-Corry Hall
Queen's University, Kingston, Ontario, Canada K7L 3N6
Tel 613 533-6318   Fax 613 533-2824

MEMORANDUM

To: **The Prime Minister of Canada**

From: **Maragret Hillyard Little** | *Anti-poverty activist and Professor of women's studies and political science, Queen's University*

Subject: **A Five-Point Plan So Single Mothers Can Hold Their Heads Up High**

Poor single mothers are vilified by our society. Along with prisoners, immigrants, and squeegee kids, poor single mothers are condemned as unworthy of our sympathy. They are blamed for what? Their poverty—and their struggles to raise the next generation of Canadian citizens.

I am an anti-poverty activist and an academic. I have interviewed single mothers about their experiences of the Canadian welfare system for more than a decade. My most recent interviews have caused me to be overwhelmingly depressed and outraged by how our country treats the unfortunate. Almost every one of the single mothers interviewed admitted that she does not eat three meals a day—she cannot afford to. In order to feed and shelter their children, they skip meals on a regular basis.

Many single mothers I meet have insecure housing. They move from place to place because they can't afford the rent; they have landlords who will reduce their rent if the women agree to have "sex on the side." I know single mothers who have returned to abusive partners because they realize that welfare will not provide enough money for them to raise their children on their own. These women are making the ultimate sacrifices in order that they can save their children from the worst of poverty.

The world already is well aware of our weak record in accommodating the poor. A couple of years ago the United Nations rapped Canada's knuckles for the growing disparity between the rich and the poor. While the study ranked Canada as the best country in the world to live in, it said that was not true if you were poor. Canada ranked tenth among seventeen industrialized nations in its treatment of the poor. That is mainly due to the way our country treats poor single mothers. An appalling 43% of all Canadian children living with single mothers are poor, while only 16% of such children are poor in Norway.

Given that women on average make 70 cents to every male dollar and that the majority of separated and divorced fathers do not pay adequate child support, it is not surprising that single mothers would be among our poorest citizens. Because they are women and because they end up with the bulk of parenting responsibilities, it is only common sense that single mothers are the most vulnerable to the ebb and flow of Canada's social policies. And certainly during the last decade Canada has gutted its social spending, a policy that has affected all Canadians but has devastated poor single mothers.

Across the country, almost every province has dramatically cut welfare rates. For example, the Harris government in Ontario cut welfare rates by 22%. That is one-fifth of poor people's income—gone overnight. I have followed the entire history of welfare in this country and these cuts in the 1990s were unprecedented. Not even during the Depression did governments cut relief and mothers' allowance rates but in the mean 1990s we decided to blame the poor for their poverty and make it impossible for them to survive.

The Impact of the Cuts

These new rates have affected every aspect of poor single mothers' lives. It has affected their nutrition. Even before the welfare rate cut in Ontario, a study demonstrated that it was impossible on a welfare income to eat according to Canada's Food Guide once you had paid your rent. I cannot tell you the number of mothers who are eating a stale muffin for supper tonight, or sending their kids to the local soup kitchen every other night.

The rate cuts have also affected housing. Canada is one of the only industrialized nations that does not have a national social housing policy. With welfare rate cuts single mothers have had to leave secure housing and turn to poorer, cheaper rental accommodation in less favourable neighbourhoods. Many have given up their phones because they can no longer afford them. One single mother I interviewed sold most of her furniture in order to feed and clothe her children.

Welfare rate cuts have also increased the violence that single mothers and their children face in daily life. The Ontario Association of Interval and Transition Houses found that more single mothers are returning to abusive partners since the welfare rate cut in Ontario was instituted because they simply cannot afford to live on their own. I have met more than one single mother who has admitted to doing the same. Because of welfare cuts women are sacrificing their own safety, putting their bodies and their lives on the line in order to feed and shelter their children.

Along with welfare rate cuts, most provincial governments have increased their policing of the poor. Employing Gestapo-like techniques, welfare administrations have done their best to increase the harassment of the poor. They have established welfare telephone fraud lines, increased house investigations, and interrogations of third parties—all to catch the welfare cheater.

But study after government study shows that welfare fraud is *not* a problem. The Harris government's own recent study of welfare fraud found 747 welfare fraud convictions in a caseload of 238,042. That means Ontario has a welfare fraud rate of 0.3%. That is indeed a low welfare fraud rate—especially when you compare it to figures of middle-class fraud reports. For instance, 25% of Canadians are believed to cheat on their income tax forms and another 22% cheat when declaring goods as they cross the border. And yet there are no province-wide telephone lines or newly hired staff to investigate these rampant fraud activities.

A Five-Point Plan

But do not lose heart. I have a five-point plan, Mr. Prime Minister, that will change all that. A plan that will make single mothers entitled Canadian citizens who will be respected for their everyday battle to feed, clothe, educate, and nurture their children.

1. WELFARE BASED SOLELY ON ECONOMIC NEED

No other criteria are necessary. In a just society we will give money to those in economic need so they can live in dignity. There will be no drug tests, no fingerprints, no job training workshops to attend—you will simply receive welfare if you can prove you are in economic need. After all, business people, students, and academics like myself all receive government money without having to endure humiliating and intrusive investigations. Why shouldn't everyone be treated the same?

That policy decision will also have the added benefit of saving provincial governments tremendous administrative costs. There will be no more welfare workers staking out parking lots at night, checking who visits the welfare mom, and no more house visits to check whether there is evidence of a man living there. Instead, welfare workers will be able to concentrate on the important task of verifying the financial need of the applicants.

2. WELFARE RATE THAT MEETS THE BASIC NEEDS OF ALL CANADIANS

As prime minister, you can insist that welfare rates across the provinces and territories meet the Low Income Cut-off Line established by your very own National Council of Welfare. This poverty line, accepted by most social policy scholars, is regionally sensitive to local costs of food, shelter, clothing, and other basic necessities. Perhaps it would sweeten the pie if you told the provinces that you would pay 50% of this welfare rate—just as you used to before you abolished the Canada Assistance Plan.

3. ABOLISH WELFARE FRAUD LINES

It is fiscally irresponsible of the provinces to continue welfare fraud telephone lines when all reports indicate that welfare fraud is extremely low and is not growing. The recovery from welfare fraud cannot be meeting the administrative costs of supporting such a program. The Manitoba government recently saw the light and abolished its welfare fraud line. You, as prime minister, can make this a stipulation of receiving federal monies for welfare programs.

4. NATIONAL RETRAINING PROGRAM DESIGNED FOR SINGLE MOTHERS

No retraining program is effective unless participants choose to participate. Again, as criteria for receiving federal support you can insist that all training programs are voluntary—that there is no coercion or financial rewards for participating in any training program. You don't need to coerce people to take training programs that lead to well-paid jobs. But most training programs involve such pressures.

Any retraining program for single mothers must permit these women to take time off work when their children are ill or having difficulties. Most retraining programs for women also lead to dead-end, low-paid, part-time work at best. Retraining programs that offer real opportunities for single mothers to get off welfare must be longer term and include life skills workshops and counselling that can help support women to make huge changes in their personal lives. To be highly effective there should also be a range of retraining for non-traditional jobs such as carpentry, mechanics, and computer technology. Those jobs pay better than most female-dominated jobs, allowing single mothers to provide their children with more opportunities.

5. NATIONAL CHILD-CARE PROGRAM

You, dear Prime Minister, have already promised a national child-care program to Canadians. Now is the time that you can keep that promise and make a brighter future for all mothers. The lack of child care is one of the greatest barriers to single mothers' participation in training programs and the workforce. You can make that problem disappear with a national, accessible, quality child-care program. Such a program will allow mothers to choose when to be at home caring for their children and when to re-enter the workforce. This is a choice that middle-class mothers make all the time—surely working-class and poor mothers should have the same choice.

With this five-point plan, I can guarantee you that single mothers will become active, proud members of society. They will be able to make effective choices about their own lives. They will be able to leave abusive relationships without fear for their survival. They will be able to provide three nutritious meals a day for themselves and their children. They will be proud of their mothering and will be financially rewarded through the welfare system for their caring work. They will be able to choose when it is appropriate to retrain and return to the workforce. They will be able to hold their heads up high and provide a future of opportunities to their children.

Fred McMahon

Fred McMahon *is director of the Social Affairs Centre at the Fraser Institute and also manages the Economic Freedom of the World project.* Mr. McMahon, who received his M.A. in economics from McGill University, has been policy director at the Toronto-based Consumer Policy Institute and senior policy analyst at the Atlantic Institute for Market Studies. He is author of *Looking the Gift Horse in the Mouth: The Impact of Federal Transfers on Atlantic Canada*, which won the Sir Anthony Fisher International Memorial Award for advancing public policy debate, and *Road to Growth: How Lagging Economies Become Prosperous*. His most recent work, *Retreat from Growth: Atlantic Canada and the Negative Sum Economy*, features an introduction by Nobel Laureate Robert Mundell.

THE FRASER INSTITUTE

M E M O R A N D U M

To: **The Prime Minister of Canada**

From: **Fred McMahon**
*Director of Social Affairs Centre
The Fraser Institute*

Subject: **End Poverty by Ending Welfare
As We Know It**

Poverty in Canada could be virtually eliminated in a generation. The policy prescription is easy. End welfare. Re-institute poorhouses and homes for unwed mothers.

That might seem like drastic action, rich in its potential for human tragedy. Society would, rightly, reject the prescription although over time it would virtually end the disease of poverty, which has afflicted humanity since the first cities arose.

Never before in human history has a person's future been less dependent on their past or family station. Never before in human history has society had the prosperity to offer comprehensive education to all citizens. Never before has society generated such wealth or such opportunity for everyone.

All the barriers people once faced—barriers that could pen people into poverty— have disappeared. Yet poverty has not disappeared, though its nature has changed. Poverty seldom means deprivation of physical necessities as in the past. This is doubtless the first generation in human history where obesity is a real health problem for the poor. But poverty in a relative sense remains with us.

HEAD OFFICE:
4th Floor, 1770 Burrard Street
Vancouver, British Columbia
Canada V6J 3G7
Phone: (604) 688-0221
Fax: (604) 688-8539
Web site:
    www.fraserinstitute.ca
E-mail:
    info@fraserinstitute.ca

TORONTO OFFICE:
Phone: (416) 363-6575
Fax: (416) 601-7322

OTTAWA OFFICE:
Phone: (603) 565-0468

CALGARY OFFICE:
301 – 815 1st Street S.W.
Calgary, Alberta
Canada T2P 1N3
Phone: (403) 216-7175
Fax: (403) 234-9010

*With strategic
alliances
in 53 countries.*

Here, I'm focusing on poverty as an economic phenomenon. There are non-economic causes of poverty, which, of course, admit no economic solution. People with physical or mental handicaps will often need help to escape poverty. Those trapped by addiction face great obstacles until they overcome their addiction.

But why, in a world bounding with possibilities, do so many normal, healthy people make poor choices that lead to poverty? Why do so many young people give up on education? Why, even as unskilled adults, do they allow themselves to get trapped into a cycle of welfare and low-skill jobs, when dozens of training programs are available? Why are others simply unable to hold jobs once they get them? Why do teenage girls have unprotected sex, when single motherhood is almost a certain route to poverty?

Poverty as Voluntary Choice

Those are questions the policy reformer—or even the most radical social activist—needs to address before prescribing solutions to the poverty problem. Given all the opportunities each of us faces, poverty is now largely a voluntary choice.

That statement will infuriate many, but it remains true that virtually no one growing up in Canada need be mired in poverty as an adult. Individuals seldom make a clear-cut decision to be poor. Instead it is usually the collective weight of a number of decisions—play is more fun than studying; if I quit school and work I can have more money than any of my friends; not to mention all the difficult sexual choices teenagers face today.

Social welfare programs are invariably set up to help people with today's problems—welfare for a single mother who can't make ends meet without government assistance, Employment

Insurance for a fisher who needs help supporting the family during the off-season. But the long-term consequences of those programs have seldom been thought out.

What happens as it becomes more acceptable socially and economically to be a single parent? What happens when the fisher's son, instead of staying in school, decides to become a fisher himself, subsidized by EI money, even though he knows the work leads to a dead-end? The cycle of poverty is perpetuated through voluntary choice.

The problem that afflicts social programs is known in economics as moral hazard—the idea that a policy meant to guard against a bad event makes the event more likely. The classic case is fire insurance. Few shop owners set fires because they have fire insurance. Similarly, few teenage girls become pregnant in order to collect welfare and get their own apartment. But it does happen in both situations.

Far more typically, moral hazard leads to a slackening of precautions—fire alarms with dead batteries, lack of care to avoid hazardous collections of inflammable materials, and sloppy electrical insulation. If fire insurance were outlawed tomorrow, by next week the number of fires would decline—at least business fires. (Presumably people have many good reasons to make their homes safe, even if they are insured.)

Similar problems afflict social programs. For example, while few women plan for single motherhood, it still may not seem that bad a fate to a young girl who wants to get out from under her parents. Government programs may well appear to promise reasonable support and independence, provided she becomes pregnant and moves out of her parents' place. The prospect becomes less worrisome if the girl has grown up in a society where single motherhood is accepted and even normal. Precautions become less important.

The safety net makes the consequences of bad choices seem more tolerable. Anti-poverty programs all too often make poverty more acceptable and thereby perpetuate it. Employment Insurance, which is now a full-blown social program in Atlantic Canada, has become a classic case of perverse results.

People treat EI as a right, not as a prop while they are looking for work. Abundant studies and anecdotal evidence reveal that most repeat EI recipients in Atlantic Canada (from where I hail) believe they have no obligation to seek or to accept work while collecting benefits. The number of recipients in Atlantic Canada typically exceeds the region's official unemployment rate. That may seem improbable but the unemployment rate is determined by Statistics Canada through a telephone poll in which only those who are looking for work and are willing to work are counted as unemployed. Yet many people collecting EI are neither seeking nor willing to accept work.

The whole work year in communities throughout Atlantic Canada is now structured to maximize the amount of EI collected. Dead-end, low-skill occupations have been subsidized and preserved by Employment Insurance. Skills, education, and training have all been negatively affected. The EI reforms of 1996, which made the system less generous, appear to have had a salutary impact. The years young people spend in school have increased, as has the number of young people who go on to technical schools, colleges, and universities, a study by Rick Audas and David Murrell found. But older people, already trapped by the system, have had little success—or interest—in finding year-round work and improving their prospects. All reform has done is reduce their income.

And there's the rub. How do you reform a social program without revictimizing the victims? How do you make single motherhood—or a life on EI—something young people will strive mightily to avoid without penalizing those trapped by the system?

Overcoming the Tradeoffs

If all welfare programs were ended tomorrow, it would be catastrophic for those who have become dependent on welfare. But far fewer people would be poor in the future. The end of welfare would eliminate the two main routes for the "inheritance" of poverty—the welfare culture and single-mother families. Ending welfare would focus young people on the need to take responsibility for their own future.

A hundred years ago a flood of immigrants and refugees arrived in North America from Eastern Europe. They came in dire poverty, often with no possessions of value at all. Many couldn't speak English. The educational opportunities for their children were limited, often because of the need to have the children working. And much of North American society was suffused with a palpable prejudice against those immigrants, particularly Jewish ones.

The succeeding generations have prospered mightily. Families knew there was no free "social assistance" lunch and the path not just to a better life but to any reasonable life at all was through hard work and education. The obstacles these immigrants—and millions of others—had to overcome hardly exist any more. Yet poverty continues.

Welfare can't be ended tomorrow, but today is not too soon to realize we need to break the self-perpetuating rotation of existing welfare programs and design new programs that won't trap future generations.

Welfare reform in the United States provides a number of pointers for the future. It has succeeded in moving millions off welfare. More speculatively, it may already be a factor behind the ongoing reduction in teen pregnancy, though it is far too early to tell its impact on long-term, deep-seated behaviours that can take a generation to change.

But again there's that tradeoff: How do you prevent people from becoming trapped without creating immense suffering for those already trapped? The return to poorhouses and homes for unwed mothers is one extreme of the tradeoff. In a generation, it would come close to eliminating poverty but only at great human cost.

Leaving welfare programs unreformed is the other extreme. We should no longer tolerate programs that foster and subsidize bad choices and perpetuate the very phenomena they are supposed to treat. Yet many social activist groups have convinced themselves that people don't have choices and that the only way to decrease poverty is to increase welfare. Bad programs don't matter because choice doesn't matter. That is absurd and only swells the numbers of the poor in the long run.

Transition policies will be necessary to help people move off welfare. The purpose of this brief memo is not to spell out these policies but rather to encourage the reader to consider the following controversial points in examining social policy:

- In today's society of great opportunity, poverty is usually a voluntary choice, though one made when young without understanding of the full consequences.
- Social programs perpetuate poverty by limiting the negative consequences of bad choices and by masking their extent.

- In the future, social programs have to be reformed so they don't subsidize bad choices.
- Social programs themselves should be structured to alert young people to the consequences of their choices.

We could virtually eliminate poverty in a generation. The human costs would be too immense. But that's no excuse for failing to understand the role anti-poverty programs play in perpetuating poverty and to use that understanding to do better in the future.

Jack Layton

Jack Layton | *is the president of the Federation of Canadian Municipalities and chairs its National Housing Policy Options team.* His work at the federation has led to the creation of a coalition of municipalities from across Canada that are working together for a renewed federal housing policy. On Toronto's council he co-chairs the Homeless Advisory Committee, which provides a vital policy link to front-line workers and people who have experienced homelessness, and authored *HOMELESS-NESS: The Making and Unmaking of a Crisis*. Layton has taught urban studies at all of Toronto's universities and is now adjunct professor in the planning program of the geography department at the University of Toronto.

Federation of
Canadian Municipalities

Fédération canadienne
des municipalités

Councillor **Jack Layton**
Toronto, Ontario

President
Président

24 rue Clarence Street
Ottawa, Ontario
K1N 5P3
phone: (613) 241-5221
fax: (613) 241-7440
federation@fcm.ca
Web site: www.fcm.ca

M E M O R A N D U M

To: **The Prime Minister of Canada**

From: **Jack Layton** | *Toronto city councillor and President, Federation of Canadian Municipalities*

Subject: **Taking Action Against Homelessness**

Ten generations ago, my shipbound ancestors were homeless, starving refugees who landed on the shores of the Petticotiak River. Seventeen families arrived on that boat, a small ocean-tossed wooden ship with Captain Monk at the helm. Moncton bears his name today near the site where they hove to. Without the warm welcome and indispensable survival advice of the Mi'kmaq First Nations residents, who generously imparted thousands of years of local survival experience despite no common language, Monk's charges would not have coped with the harsh winter conditions. Without the Aboriginal values and spirit that compelled assistance to those in need, there would not be over 300,000 descendants of my family in North America.

What a contrast today, when descendants of our hosts are homeless in winter and craving warmth, lying over the sewer grates of our city sidewalks or crammed into shelters. Reserve housing falls so far below any standard elsewhere in the country that aboriginal poverty and its fallout include staggeringly high infant mortality rates, incidence of disease, and low life expectancy.

We are doing precisely the opposite to our First Nations brothers and sisters as they did to us when we arrived in need. We have no national housing strategy to help reduce First Nations' homelessness in our communities—and in this respect, of course, First Nations poor are not alone. As I type these words, there is no operational national affordable housing strategy for *anyone* in Canada. True, Aboriginal housing conditions are magnitudes worse than any other single segment of the population of this land, but hundreds of thousands of Canadians from many backgrounds suffer homelessness each year. Steadily growing poverty and rapidly increasing housing costs are intersecting right in the middle of the daily lives of a growing number of Canadians.

A chilling landscape is laid out by government reports, studies by academics and front-line charities working with the homeless, and the testimonials of the homeless themselves. Across Canada, upwards of 800,000 households face gut-wrenching financial hardships as the housing affordability crisis deepens and they are forced to pay out more than 50% of their income in skyrocketing rents.

It's a crisis, but one that can be ended if we act together—as history shows.

Do you remember, Prime Minister, when alarm bells sounded about the poverty gap a generation ago? House of Commons debates and even a Senate study focused attention on poverty because a growing number of our fellow citizens had to devote over 25% of their annual incomes to housing. A war on poverty was declared to address that emergency. New national social programs were combined with a national affordable-housing construction agenda. From the fertile combination of federal funding and community elbow grease grew bricks and mortar, roof trusses and bathroom tiles, seniors' apartments, new communities of town homes, and even highrises. Tens of thousands of homes were built in two decades.

Twenty years later, the United Nations even gave Canada an award for its advanced housing policies for those in need. That award was given in 1993, but someone should have told the smiling UN officials to keep the award. After all, 1993 was the same year that the newly elected Liberal government drove a stake through the very housing policies being honoured. Housing and social assistance both fell under the mesmerizing and omnipotent budgetary axe. It was an axe that viciously chopped long-held values of compassion, equality, assistance to those in need, and economic justice. It was an axe driven by the muscled arms of the free-market mantra.

Now in the early years of the twenty-first century, there are so many Canadian tenant households—over 2.5 million—paying over 25% of their income in rent that we are forced to focus instead on the people who are the worst hit, those paying over half their monthly incomes to their landlords just to keep a roof over their heads. Mere dollars away from homelessness in any given month, those citizens turn to food banks, do without food altogether to make sure that kids get enough, and give up visits to friends or even doctors because transit fares break their budgets. Despite those efforts, more and more Canadians are becoming homeless.

Please, Prime Minister, don't join those who charge that the homeless "want" to be on the streets. My travels in Canadian streets have found no evidence for such rhetoric. Freezing deaths now dot the records of coroners across the country (almost one individual per week in Toronto alone). Believe me, the homeless do not want to meet such fates. Blaming victims is the last refuge for adherents of an emergent, callous value system in the Canadian polity. Don't go there.

And please don't hide behind the argument that housing won't help people who have become homeless because they face a multitude of problems, such as addictions and mental health problems. Afraid that you might resuscitate compassion and justice in Canadian social policy, backroom whisperers and editorialists alike try to persuade you that "homelessness really isn't the problem. We just need better coordination of services for the ailments these unfortunates suffer. Then they'll be all right."

Listen instead to the wise advice of an ex-addict that was offered to me recently in the vestibule of a new affordable housing complex built in Vancouver's downtown east side by the province, the city, and community groups: "Without that roof over your head, you can't even start on the road back!" He's right. The common foundation of the homelessness experience is the lack of a roof, which your government can pay for. The way forward starts right there.

When you are prime minister, you have to ask Canadians to put aside their stereotypes—like the images of the homeless of old: a few fellows sipping from brown bags on city park benches. New realities face us today: low-income seniors and women with their children are the most rapidly growing group of homeless Canadians. In some cities, like Calgary and Fort McMurray, many in homeless shelters are actually working people—they simply cannot afford the scant available housing in those boomtowns.

Some advisors may be telling you that homelessness is just a problem of a couple of big cities and Canadians would object if the federal government were seen to be providing extra resources to rich places like Toronto. But many towns across this country have been opening shelters for the homeless—church basements with mats and meals. No part of this land is immune.

In the fall of 1998, prompted by community groups working with the homeless, mayors from across Canada went so far as to declare "homelessness and the affordable housing crisis to be a national disaster." Their declaration called on your government, Prime Minister, to join with communities across the country in creating a massive national affordable housing strategy. Some of the mayors were fresh from the Quebec ice storm and the Manitoba floods, which saw unprecedented mobilization of Canadians' concern and resources to help those in need. They asked, "Where was that national energy and commitment when faced with thousands in homeless shelters and on streets day-in and day-out?"

Not content to mouth rhetoric, the mayors and their councils—from Victoria to Halifax to Whitehorse—set to work designing an affordable housing plan. Coordinated through their national organization, the Federation of Canadian Municipalities, the plan was intentionally modest: "Let's commit to reducing the homelessness and affordable housing crisis by half in a decade." No one, Prime Minister, could suggest that ten years to solve half of a serious problem like homelessness would be moving too fast!

No doubt as you are about to agree with me you are also, however, remembering the provinces. You're remembering the Social Union Framework Agreement and the fact the provinces wanted Ottawa to download housing to them, along with large sums of federal dollars with no strings attached. The download was done, with a portion of the requested cash. I can hear you say, "The federal government lost interest in that whole policy area. Do we really want to get back in?"

It's true that achieving even our modest target, the federation found, would require significant national resources. But those would not be out of line with the funds devoted to affordable housing solutions in other advanced and democratic nations. The total cost of the ten-year program, $1.7 billion per year with matching provincial dollars and participation by municipal governments and community groups, would amount to roughly 1% of the budget of our governments.

The program has three prime components. First, we need to build 20,000 new homes per year that would be affordable to those who are paying more than 50% of their incomes in rent per year and are at risk of homelessness. That would mean 200,000 households would be accommodated by this new housing at the end of the decade.

Second, each year 10,000 units of the slum-like substandard housing that has sprung up in too many communities need to be rehabilitated for those with low incomes, who in most cases already live in them. Underlining that need was the reminder by Winnipeg mayor Glen Murray that thirty-six people died in fires in dangerous decrepit housing in a mere twenty-four months in his community. A useful policy called the Residential Rehabilitation Programme could serve as the basis of this plan but would need significant expansion if it were to break through the needs. This part of our proposed agenda would give Canada's homeless and underhoused 100,000 fixed-up and affordable homes over a ten-year time frame.

Finally, for many of the people paying over 50% of their income in rent, it makes sense to help them stay in the homes in which they currently live. Such a policy of rental assistance would relieve financial hardship with the least disruption to families and at the least cost to taxpayers. The federation recommended that a total of 400,000 households need to be receiving this assistance within ten years in order to cut the affordable housing crisis in half.

Housing policy—or more accurately, the lack of housing policy in Canada—is revealing flaws in our current system of federalism. We've seen some of these flaws before—in the medicare mess, for example—where struggles, jealousies, and political partisanship between federal and provincial leaders block solutions like a bad case of constipation. Perhaps as you consider taking action on housing it would be a good time to consider a reordering of the relationships between governments in this country.

Municipalities and their local communities are ready to roll up their sleeves and deal with homelessness. They have proven it with modest but innovative projects from coast to coast. Their problem is resources. Municipalities would be building affordable housing today in significant quantities, I'm sure, but they take in only 4.5% of the tax revenue of this country while provinces and your national government collect 95.5%.

What's needed is a recasting of Canada's dysfunctional governmental partnership—and especially a new recognition of the role of municipal governments. When final authority over municipalities was enshrined with the provinces in the *British North America Act*, the population was about 90% rural and

10% urban. Today, over 80% of Canadians live in urban areas. It's time for cities and communities to be freed to engage in the solutions that our country needs—and to be given the resources to do so.

A covenant to work with municipalities on the raw edges of services to the homeless has begun to emerge through the Supporting Community Partnerships Initiative under the purview of federal minister Claudette Bradshaw. We need similar models to work on a much larger scale for the construction of housing across the land. The municipalities are ready. Let those provinces who wish to join us do so, but don't permit any of them, Prime Minister, to veto your joining with communities in building solutions.

This would be a national partnership to mobilize Canada's resources through local solutions. Localism is an effective response to the harsh anonymity of globalism and an antidote to its excesses. A national affordable housing plan is needed now. Let's act, together.

Roger L. Martin

Roger L. Martin | *is the dean of the Joseph L. Rotman School of Management at the University of Toronto.* Previously, he was a director of Monitor Company, a strategy consulting firm based in Cambridge, Massachusetts; he also served as co-head of the company in 1995 and 1996, with responsibility for its day-to-day activities and over 700 consultants worldwide. A Canadian from Wallenstein, Ontario, he joined Monitor in 1985 and two years later founded the firm's Toronto office. Mr. Martin received his A.B. from Harvard College, with a concentration in economics, in 1979 and his M.B.A. from the Harvard Business School in 1981.

Rotman

MEMORANDUM
Roger L. Martin
Dean

105 St. George Street
Toronto, Ontario
M5S 3E6
www.rotman.utoronto.ca

M E M O R A N D U M

To: **The Prime Minister of Canada**

From: **Roger L. Martin** | *Dean,*
Joseph L. Rotman School of Management

Subject: **What Canada Could be for Education
in the Twenty-First Century**

As we move into the twenty-first century, knowledge and skills—what we think of as human capital—will become the critical determinants in the economic success of both nations and individuals.

When your predecessor Wilfrid Laurier proclaimed almost one hundred years ago that the twentieth century would belong to Canada, he was basing his claim on Canada's abundance of natural resources. Canada in the twenty-first century can go beyond its traditional role as a purveyor of natural resources. If we make the right strategic investments in education at all levels, Canada can not only prosper and succeed, but also will become a leader in the global economy. Innovation is the key to competitive advantage in the new world order, and intellectual capital is the coveted new currency. Investing in education is no longer a social choice; it is an economic imperative for our nation's survival.

Government needs to put a premium on education at all levels, from pre-school to postgraduate. But more of the same and increased spending alone won't cut it. We need a profound values shift and a radical reinvention if we are to lead the world in the creation of the most valued commodity in the coming century: knowledge assets—or, more particularly, what we at the Rotman School call "integrative thinkers."

Creating the best education system in the world won't be easy. Globalization, the rise of technology, and a greater emphasis on the autonomy of the individual mean we need to think about education in new ways. In the new millennium, the world will be an increasingly interconnected place. We need to look at education holistically—as a total system with continuity through all levels. Right now, we are doing the opposite.

We do not teach students to see the world as an interconnected place. We do not teach students to see the big view, to think integratively. We do not teach them to function in a complex world.

The fundamental educational experience of our students now is that they learn in silos—English separate from Math which in turn is cut off from History—right from kindergarten, a stale curriculum that does not connect to the society in which students actually live and function. We can't produce integrative thinkers with a non-integrative machine.

Why do we teach our children to think in silos and not integratively?

There is actually some sense to it, but plenty of nonsense as well.

On the sense side, the world of knowledge is vast. We can't expect everyone to tackle it like a Renaissance scholar. And in fact if we did, we would confuse and demotivate the vast majority of students. In the terminology of learning scholar James March, we pursue simplification and specialization to handle the complexity of the challenge of learning in a vast sea of knowledge. As such, a critical part of education involves breaking the interconnected world into chunks—simplification—that can be tackled and mastered one by one: specialization. That makes sense. Our students need to gain mastery, and mastery is achieved more quickly with simplification.

On the nonsense side, we have become so comfortable with the drive for mastery that we have forgotten in the educational world about the interconnectedness. We simplify and implicitly believe that multiple specializations will educate our students well. That is, if we provide them with a wide assortment of simplified subjects—seven to ten at a time during elementary and secondary school, four or five at a time at university—we will provide students the insights on interconnectedness that we take away through simplification into educational silos.

That is where the fallacy lies. Side-by-side learning of topics does not equate to integrative learning. Understanding how to integrate across models in order to build a meta-model is as much an area requiring knowledge and mastery as is arithmetic, chemistry, marketing, or torts. Across the world of education, we don't teach mastery of integration. As a result, students learn how to simplify and specialize but not how to integrate.

The adverse consequences are numerous. As students practise simplification and specialization, they become blind to the need to integrate, in due course seeing the world in silos. As a consequence, they find the interconnected world more complicated and worrisome than they would if they had integrative skills. M.B.A. graduates, for example, reorganize the assembly line for efficiency, following what they learned in operations management, and are perplexed when the workers revolt, even though they learned something about employee satisfaction and morale in human resource management. Rather than understanding and mastering the real and interconnected world in which they live, they attempt to continue viewing it through the simplified lens we have taught them.

Perhaps most problematically, they do not learn to deal productively with model clash. Integrative thinking teaches students that models clash all the time and that the work of a thinker is to build new models that overcome the clash. For the M.B.A. graduate above, the integrative challenge is building a meta-model of efficiency that takes into account what mastery in operations management and mastery in human resources management bring into direct conflict. Current education teaches students that when models clash it is a big problem, not a nifty challenge to overcome, and that the task is to pick one model over the other and accept the inevitable consequences.

The integrative thinker is a relentless learner who seeks to develop a repertoire of skills to enable him or her to engage the tensions between opposites long enough to transcend duality and seek novel solutions. The integrative thinker develops a stance that embraces rather than fears the essential qualities of enigmatic choices. Integrative thinkers understand that learning is an art—a heuristic process, not an algorithm with pat or formulaic answers. In short, integrative thinking is the educational paradigm we need to adopt if we are to produce citizens capable of processing and responding to the rapid change and complexity that will characterize our world in the coming century.

Creating an education system that can produce integration is no small task. Right now, as the world changes rapidly and our stale educational bureaucracy refuses to change, young people are ahead of us. Unlike their teachers, principals, and university administrators, they are dialled in to the Internet and they are already connected to a global bank of knowledge and people that is starting to make their school experience seem less and less relevant. Many of them no longer bother with studying and extra-curricular activities, but are participating in the real world by working after school and communicating globally over the Internet.

We need to bring these young Canadians back to the class-room by designing an education system that fosters creative and integrative thinking. Doing so will not only create great knowledge assets for Canada—it will also be how we will attract the century's most coveted resources from other parts of the globe. In a world where people can work anywhere, through the Internet, who wouldn't want to raise their family in a beautiful northern country with the best education system in the world?

What company wouldn't want to locate where the world's best thinkers are trained, near to universities with the best research, and the best ability to innovate?

The difference in producing citizens under such an education system would be dramatic. Integrative education teaches our citizens that models routinely clash and that when they do, the hard and fun work has just begun. When these citizens come into conflict—I think x and you think not x—they have a skill-set and a propensity for creating an answer that creatively resolves the difference. Traditional education teaches our citizens that when models clash, they have an insuperable problem and the choice is to produce a winner and a loser.

Integrative education creates continuous learning and the building of ever more powerful models of understanding our interconnected world. Traditional education perpetuates a world that can be nasty, brutish, short. Canada's role in the world should be as an educational beacon for the former, not a contributor to the sorry rule of the latter.

Better education in Canada not only means a bright economic future here, it means a better world. Our citizens will be healthier, more likely to be employed, and more likely to participate in a civic society. But it will also mean that as a society we are ready to participate and lead in an increasingly complex world. Helping young people learn to think integratively will not only produce better students, better future employees, and better thinkers, it will also produce compassionate world citizens, with a view big enough that we can trust them to be the custodians of our fragile planet.

If we invest in this, Prime Minister, the twenty-first century could belong to Canada in a way that none of your predecessors could ever have imagined. We will not only help create a just society in Canada, we will perhaps help create, for the first time in history, the hope of a just society in the world.

Gail Bowen

Gail Bowen, *associate professor and head of the English department at Saskatchewan Indian Federated College,* has received widespread acclaim for her award-winning detective series featuring Joanne Kilbourn, a fictional character who has much in common with her creator. Ms. Bowen has had four of her plays produced at Regina's Globe Theatre—*Dancing in Poppies, Beauty and the Beast, the Tree,* and an adaptation of Peter Pan. Born in Toronto, she learned to read by age three from tombstones in Prospect Cemetery, which came in handy when she was struck by polio two years later. She was educated at the University of Toronto, University of Waterloo, and the University of Saskatchewan.

MEMORANDUM

To: The Prime Minister of Canada

From: **Gail Bowen** | *Author and head of English,
Saskatchewan Indian Federated College*

Subject: **The Art of the Jitterbug:
Balancing Work and Family**

Two years ago a friend who happened to be our province's deputy minister of labour asked me to co-chair a conference on balancing work and family. She assured me the duties were not onerous. All I had to do was show up, introduce the speakers who had done the real work, and keep the program rolling along. I agreed because I'm very fond of my friend and because the topic was of more than academic interest to me.

My husband and I had spent years handing off babies at the door as we headed to graduate classes or later to teach. Now the first of those babies and her partner had two small children of their own, and we were watching them confront a task with which we were only too familiar: keeping all the balls in the air at once.

Yogi Berra would have said it was a case of "déjà vu all over again," but for once, Yogi would have been wrong. Things had changed for young parents. In the 1970s my husband and I saw juggling work and family as a purely personal concern, an off-shoot of the fact that we had both chosen to study, to work, and to raise children. If it took longer to complete our degrees, if we had to work for lower salaries for a longer time, we were pre-pared to accept the tradeoff. Ours was a deliberate, personal decision, one we saw few other couples making. Certainly we would never have pled for special consideration or understand-ing from either colleagues or employers. We were on our own.

Our daughter, Hildy, and her partner were not. Thanks to an enlightened employer, our daughter brought both her little girls to her workplace for the first six months of their lives. Probably the only creature in the world more in need of constant atten-tion than a newborn baby is a movie producer, but Hildy and her colleagues "balanced work and the family" as the needs arose. In fact, the standard, only half-joking line in the office when the phone rang was "It's Toronto—you take the baby." The arrangement succeeded because, like her parents twenty-eight years before her, Hildy was determined it would succeed. But this time, she and her partner were not acting alone.

A Pressing Social Issue

Two generations and two methods of coping with the demands of raising and of feeding a family. Both were adequate; both were arrived at without the benefit of government or collective bargaining.

Since I hit the age of fifty, I have become famously reluc-tant about having my consciousness raised, but as I listened to the participants at the Conference on Balancing Work and the Family, I knew it was time I came out of the closet. What I had seen before as an individual concern, I learned was anything but. What I had assumed was a family's responsibility I now saw was a pressing social issue. In the conference room that day, 500 people came together to define a systemic workplace problem, to identify the social and economic costs of that problem, and to propose workable solutions. It felt good to be there. I was proud that once again my home of Saskatchewan was functioning as Canada's social laboratory. And I was grati-fied to see that what had been a personal challenge to me as a young parent was now the concern of a significant group of opinion makers. The conclusion of the men and women who came together that day was unanimous: The first decade of the new century had to be about workplace innovations that would help employees strike a reasonable balance between the demands of work and family life. As I left the conference centre that day, I kept thinking of the old hipster comedian Lord Buckley's description of an epiphany: "It was just like the jitterbug; it was so simple it evaded me!"

But, if acknowledging the need was so simple, why had it taken us all of the previous century just to get to the place where we were ready to talk about it? If we can't answer the question of timing, we can at least point out the problem and offer some solutions.

The problem is easy to define. The traditional family dynamic of one parent at home and one at work no longer exists. In fact, one can argue that the idea of the "stay-at-home mom" is a temporary aberration of the 1950s and 1960s, as does Stephanie Coontz in her book *The Way We Really Are*. Regardless, the simple fact is that the majority of those family members who have traditionally been in charge of looking after either children or elderly parents (or both) are now in the paid work force. If there is change in the workplace because of computerization and globalization—which everyone talks about—there is equal pressure from near universal participation in the work force, which is less discussed.

Some argue that the solution is simply to convince women to get back in the home where they belong. We could dignify that viewpoint with a rebuttal, but in reality we would be wasting our time, because the fact is we are not going back. The trend toward the dual-earner family is irreversible. Women—and men—are staying in the work force because they want to be there, even if money was not an object; and money is an important object. By 1989, for instance, almost 80% of all homebuyers came from two-income households. Further, a recent study shows that it takes seventy-seven weeks of paid employment at average wages to cover the expenses of a typical Canadian family.

Inevitably, the fact that more and more couples are working while simultaneously trying to meet their family responsibilities leads to tensions. Once it was thought that the solution to work stress was simply effective time management; today we know that no matter how efficiently we parcel out our time, we still come up short. On any given day, two people who work outside the home might need to get children up, fed, dressed, and out the door; deliver an aging parent to a doctor's appointment; shop for groceries; pick up dry-cleaning; drive kids to a softball practice; arrange for after-school child care; attend a parent-teacher meeting and be home in time to cook dinner, attend a recital, help kids with homework, and check and respond to their own office voicemail and e-mail. Little wonder that we fall into bed at night exhausted and wake unrefreshed.

The Economic Link

What are the costs of not resolving work-family conflict and tension? Here are a few facts. Statistics Canada estimates that stress-related disorders cost Canadian businesses $12 billion a year. The Vanier Institute estimates that at least a quarter of human-resource challenges are caused by home/work conflicts. A U.S. study says that over 200 million working days are lost every year because of stress, a major cause being inadequate child care. Inadequate work performance, increased absenteeism, high turnover rates, and poor morale have all been linked to the conflict between home and work.

Policies that lead to stronger families are no longer a "feel good" issue. From a hard-nosed business perspective, they are necessary because they have a direct impact on the productivity and competitiveness of companies and of societies. So I may be arguing for the "soft side," as they say these days in government, but I am also arguing a dollars and cents issue, the hard side. As is so often the case, the two sides need not be at loggerheads.

What is good for one is good for the other.

In other words—and this is so self-evident it seems to me that it only needs to be stated to be believed—raising kids and caring for elders is valuable work. Those undertakings are important intrinsically and they are necessary if we are to have a civilized and productive society. As Daniel Keating and Fraser Mustard have argued, "Our future economic prosperity depends ... on the diversity of talent society has available. Failure to invest in families with children thus has potential costs. Adequate support improves the prospects for future economic growth." Those nags to our social conscience, European countries, have known this for years and have acted on it. It is now our turn.

So we have a serious problem easy to define: not a woman's issue but a labour and social issue. Are the solutions as easy? Of course they never are, but there are some attitudes we can begin to work on as a culture, and there are some practical steps we can take in the workplace. Changing attitude is difficult, but we can start; a few workplace adjustments shouldn't be that tough, considering the benefits.

Attitude first. We must begin by changing our profile of the ideal employee. The worker who believes that he or she owes the company a twelve-hour day and a weekend spent catching up on workplace tasks should be pitied, not venerated. Conversely, the employee who balances his work commitment with commitment to family and community should be praised, not censured. How hard would it be for our culture to redefine the word "slacker" to mean one who avoids half his or her responsibilities? Yet if we are to have a truly healthy economy, that linguistic leap must be made.

Practically, the idea of the factory whistle indicating the start of the shift is as archaic as bustles. Why should a parent whose child is picked up by the school bus at 8:15 a.m. have to be at work at 8:00? What's wrong with flextime? With adjusted lunch times? For that matter, what's wrong with some paid time off for trips to the dentist, doctor, or recital? The productivity

and loyalty the company would receive in return would far outweigh some lost minutes on the clock.

As well, if couples are committed to being in the work force,
why not allow for easier departure and re-entry: to have and
begin raising a child, to care for an elder in the last days, or just
to take a breather? Or less dramatically, what is wrong with
shared or half-time jobs?

None of these suggestions requires heavy-handed government intervention, although it is reasonable to expect enlightened governments to take a lead role with their own employees
and with enabling labour legislation. The benefits of these
adjustments will be as dramatic and life-altering as the negative
consequences I mentioned earlier. The positive changes, however, demand a collective will by employees and employers.

The real question is not "Can we do it?" but "Can we afford
not to?" Balancing the rewards of work with the joys of family
life is one jitterbug we must no longer evade.

Allan Blakeney

Allan Blakeney, *a former premier of Saskatchewan, is a visiting scholar with the College of Law at the University of Saskatchewan.* A native of Nova Scotia, Mr. Blakeney joined the public service of Saskatchewan in 1950 and served as secretary of Crown Corporations and later as chairman of the Saskatchewan Securities Commission. He was elected to the Saskatchewan Legislature in 1960 and re-elected in subsequent elections until his retirement in 1988, serving as minister of education, provincial treasurer, and minister of health as well as premier. Since his retirement he has taught at several universities, served as a director with a number of Canadian corporations and non-governmental organizations, and is currently president of the Canadian Civil Liberties Association. He received his B.A. and L.L.B. degrees from Dalhousie University and attended Oxford University on a Rhodes Scholarship, receiving B.A. and M.A. degrees.

MEMORANDUM

To: **The Prime Minister of Canada**

From: **Allan Blakeney** | *Former Premier of Saskatchewan, and visiting scholar, College of Law, University of Saskatchewan*

Subject: **Some Solutions on Aboriginal Issues**

Many Canadians are familiar with the bare bones of the issues surrounding relations between Aboriginal and non-Aboriginal people in Canada. I'd like to probe deeper, and offer some potential solutions that might be pursued by non-Aboriginal governments and organizations. I will not, however, deal with the specific legislative changes required in the *Indian Act* and otherwise.

The first thing to note is that while Aboriginal people share some common attributes they are very far from homogeneous. Non-Aboriginal Canadians, as we well know, have very different histories, ranges of experience, social and cultural situations, and economic prospects. The same is true of Aboriginal Canadians. But the differences between Aboriginal Canadians and non-Aboriginal Canadians are such that it will require conscious effort on the part of each group to improve Aboriginal/non-Aboriginal relations in Canada.

I start from the premise that Canadian governments cannot solve all or most of the problems facing Aboriginal Canadians. Aboriginal people as groups or as individuals will deal with their own problems. Frequently, however, they will require government action and support. Another important starting point, of course, is that Aboriginal people in Canada do not, as a group, occupy high positions on the socioeconomic ladder, although some Aboriginal people certainly do. Action is needed.

In developing solutions, it's helpful to divide Aboriginal peoples into three categories: northern, southern urban, and southern rural. Northern refers to Aboriginal people in the Northwest Territories, Nunavut, and, for some purposes, Yukon. Southern urban denotes Aboriginal people who live as minorities in cities and towns in the provinces, while southern rural applies to Aboriginal people who live on reserves or in predominantly Métis settlements.

My solutions fall into two broad classifications:

a. Issues of Aboriginal governance: changes in Aboriginal government structures, broadly defined, that would help Aboriginal people manage their problems.

b. Issues of economic, cultural, and social development.

Northern Aboriginals

GOVERNANCE

For northern Aboriginal people I would attempt to create territories in the Northwest Territories and Nunavut where Aboriginal people are in a substantial numerical majority. That could involve moving the border of Alberta north to include the towns of Pine Point and Hay River in order to increase the proportion of Aboriginal residents of the Northwest Territories. In these areas, approaches to Aboriginal self-government can be pursued through standard territorially based forms of government with which non-Aboriginal Canadians are reasonably familiar.

ECONOMIC, CULTURAL, AND SOCIAL

Both the federal and territorial governments should seek to

a. Add to the opportunities for northern Aboriginal people to strengthen their cultural roots.

b. Add to the economic base: proportion of the population can still make a living in the traditional ways. That includes not only hunting, fishing, and trapping but also the quasi-traditional pursuits of sports guiding and creating and selling Aboriginal art and crafts. Where mainstream economic enterprises are set up, such as mining of diamonds and other minerals, it should be carried out in a way that offers the largest possible number of jobs for local residents and allows them to retain their contacts with their local communities. A model for consideration is the manner in which uranium mining in northern Saskatchewan has been handled—with one-week-in, one-week-out work schedules, and fly-in arrangements from many Aboriginal communities.

c. Greatly strengthen opportunities for mainstream education so that those wishing to pursue a living in the mainstream are equipped to take senior jobs in government and in new economic enterprises in the north or can also go south to pursue their careers. As with other Canadians, providing varied career opportunities to northern Aboriginals is of great importance. Young Inuit and Metis people will have as their heroes skilled hunters of caribou and moose but also Susan Aglukark, George Erasmus, and other leaders who have starred on the national stage.

Southern Urban Aboriginals

The number of southern urban Aboriginal people is increasing rapidly. Many Aboriginal people are now living in towns and, in particular, our larger cities such as Vancouver, Calgary, Edmonton, Regina, Saskatoon, Winnipeg, Toronto, and Montreal. Birth rates have been high and the progeny of city-dwelling aboriginal people have only loose connections with individual bands and reserves or northern homes. Additionally, there is a steady movement from reserves to the urban centres, given that most reserves offer little economic opportunity for their residents, especially younger ones.

GOVERNANCE

Many ethnic groups in cities help to preserve their shared history, arts, and myths through social clubs, festivals, and other public events. Aboriginal people should be assisted in using similar organizations to support their cultures.

But the federal government and a couple of provinces should go further. I would like to see, say, Manitoba establish with federal assistance in Winnipeg an Aboriginal social service delivery board, an Aboriginal school board, and an Aboriginal housing board, each elected by Aboriginal residents of that city. Aboriginal people would select themselves for the purposes of participation.

The social service delivery board would deliver child welfare services, services for senior citizens, and some income assistance services. The Aboriginal school board would operate schools in somewhat the same manner as Roman Catholic separate schools and language-based Francophone and Anglophone schools are operated in some provinces. Similarly, the housing board would run a rental-housing corporation. Several such Aboriginal housing corporations have operated housing units for the Saskatchewan Housing Corporation for many years.

Those ventures would allow greater general control by Aboriginal people over their own destiny in urban centres. The boards would reduce the alienation and sense of disconnectedness many Aboriginal people feel in our major cities. It would not be easy to operate the systems since client bases might vary from year to year and there would be many different traditions among Aboriginal people of different bands, tribes, and language groups to be reconciled. As well, some Aboriginal leaders would resist such approaches since it would require Aboriginal people to identify themselves as Aboriginal rather than as Cree or Ojibway or members of, say, the Roseau

River band or first nation. Finally, some of this effort would wither if Aboriginal people entered the mainstream for social services, schooling, and housing. But we cannot predict when, or if, that will happen. So long as the structures I am proposing are kept flexible, it would offer real opportunity for improving relations between Aboriginals and non-Aboriginals in our major cities.

ECONOMIC, CULTURAL, AND SOCIAL

In strengthening economic opportunities for southern urban Aboriginal people, I would put my chief reliance on education. Prairie Indians are fond of saying, "Education is our new buffalo. We once relied on the buffalo. We must now rely on education." There is truth in that maxim.

Moreover, people in government are familiar with prescriptions for more education. There is no problem, it is frequently argued, that cannot be solved by more education. Such claims are overblown but not nonsense. In Saskatchewan we have seen a real change in the position of Aboriginal people since the 1970s when the Saskatchewan Indian Federated College, the Indian cultural and community colleges, the Métis-controlled Gabriel Dumont Institute, and the traditional faculties at the universities began turning out dozens and then hundreds of Aboriginal graduates annually.

Universities in cities with large Aboriginal populations must find ways to make their institutions more Aboriginal friendly. That won't happen quickly but results can be seen in a couple of decades. We are already seeing increases in the number of lawyers, teachers, social workers, and—more recently—engineers, health care workers, and the like who are taking their place in national and provincial affairs. Many would hope that in the fullness of time the special institutions and faculties would become defined by what they teach rather than whom they teach. We can allow that challenge to be met in the future.

I also favour conventional affirmative action programs in urban areas to increase the number of Aboriginal people in public positions. As a non-Aboriginal citizen, I believe that I have a right to see some Aboriginal visible minority faces in the public service I pay for. I believe that helps—indeed, it helps a great deal—in dealing sensibly with other public issues that concern me and cost me money.

Southern Rural

The number of southern rural Aboriginal people is declining as a percentage of the total number of Aboriginal people but it is still a large group. They are certainly the most influential element of the Aboriginal community, particularly in dealing with governments, because the Indian leadership is made up almost exclusively of people who come from reserves. The Assembly of First Nations chooses its leadership from the chiefs of bands centred on the reserves of Canada.

GOVERNANCE

It will be a real challenge to make effective Aboriginal self-government an attainable goal on reserves. Moreover, we won't make progress toward that objective unless band governments are responsive to the people whom they serve. Perhaps the best way to accomplish that is by giving band councils directly the power to tax band members. If band members don't have enough income to pay taxes it would make sense for the federal government to decrease the money transferred to band councils directly and increase the money paid out to band members on reserves, having the band council tax it back. The extra administration would be more than compensated for by the extra accountability.

ECONOMIC, CULTURAL, AND SOCIAL

The Royal Commission on Aboriginal Peoples dealt with the position of Indians on reserves in some detail. They highlighted the cultural aspects of reserve life and I believe under-emphasized the need for reserves to have some solid economic base if they are to retain and sustain large numbers of Indians as residents. The recent book by Alan Cairns, Citizens Plus, makes this case effectively.

It is not realistic to believe that the reserves can be expanded in area and economic potential to provide a solid economic base for a growing population of on-reserve Indians. A doubling of the size of reserves in provinces might have some useful impact, but it would not stem the movement off reserves and anything more than that would be difficult to achieve.

Accordingly, Aboriginal people on reserves and in majority Aboriginal communities, need the opportunity to equip themselves to operate in the economic mainstream. That is tough slugging but it is happening. Looked at over a twenty-five year period, a huge leap forward in education and in commercial involvement has occurred. The Meadow Lake Tribal Council in Saskatchewan, for example, operates an impressive commercial empire and has done so for quite a few years. So I do not despair.

Several public reports have documented how the Canadian justice system is failing Aboriginal people. Many of the recommendations have yet to be considered. It is time to act, applying some of the ideas. Separate on-reserve systems work in the United States. While circumstances are different in Canada, we should not be less timid in tackling this pressing issue.

Conclusion

There is no magic elixir to solve the problems of Aboriginal/non-Aboriginal relations. But as those Aboriginal people who wish to become more and more a part of the economic mainstream—either individually or as groups, in the way Hutterite colonies do—and as Aboriginal people decide to participate more fully in mainstream government or in Aboriginal self-government institutions, at their option, I see the development of increasingly satisfactory relations between Aboriginal and non-Aboriginal peoples in Canada.

Robert Hornung

Robert Hornung, *Policy Director at the Pembina Institute,* has worked on the climate change issue for ten years in government and environmental organizations. He has participated in many national climate change consultation processes and now sits on the national Climate Change Integrative Table, as well as serving as a member of the steering committee of the Canadian Climate Action Network, the steering committee of the Greenhouse Gas Emissions Reduction Trading Pilot, and a member of the National Advisory Committee on Energy Efficiency. Mr. Hornung holds an M.A. in political science from the University of Toronto, an Honours B.A. in political studies from Trent University, and an International Baccalaureate from Lester B. Pearson College of the Pacific.

Pembina Institute for Appropriate Development

Box 7558, Drayton Valley, AB T7A 1S7   124 O'Connor Street, Suite 505, Ottawa, ON K1P 5M9
Phone: (780) 542-6272   Fax: (780) 542-6464   Phone: (613) 235-6288   Fax: (613) 235-8118
Web site: http://www.pembina.org   email: info@pembina.org

Robert Hornung
Policy Director
Pembina Institute

M E M O R A N D U M

To: **The Prime Minister of Canada**

From: **Robert Hornung** | *Policy Director,*
       Pembina Institute

Subject: **The Need for Canadian Leadership
in Climate Change Solutions**

It is now clear that climate change represents the most significant environmental challenge facing humanity in the twenty-first century. The recent Third Assessment Report of the Intergovernmental Panel on Climate Change concluded that human activities, primarily the combustion of carbon-based fossil fuels for energy, have already begun to disrupt the global climate. Looking to the future, the panel has indicated that failure to rapidly reduce global emissions of greenhouse gases to below 50% of today's levels will have devastating impacts on global ecosystems and economies.

Canada's northerly latitude increases its vulnerability to climate change. In fact, we are already seeing clear evidence of its effects in the Arctic, where there is now 40% less sea ice in late summer than forty years ago. Permafrost is melting throughout the north, threatening human settlements and infrastructure. Melting of the entire Arctic Ocean is now a real possibility, spelling disaster for species like the polar bear.

According to Canadian scientists, greenhouse gas emissions over the next few decades could eventually cause an extensive reduction in the size of Canada's boreal forest. Water levels in the Great Lakes are projected to fall by half a metre to two metres, with significant implications for shipping and the production of hydroelectricity. Increases in drought frequency and intensity in the Canadian Prairies could impose significant costs on Canadian agriculture. All told, climate change threatens to dramatically disrupt Canada's ecosystems and the economic activity that depends on them.

While the potential impacts of climate change on Canada should make us a leader in the search for climate change solutions, we are in reality falling rapidly behind our competitors in preparing for a carbon-constrained future. Instead of declining, our greenhouse gas emissions increased by 15% between 1990 and 1999 and are currently projected to increase to 27% above 1990 levels by the year 2010. At the same time that other countries are aggressively supporting new investments in energy efficiency and renewable energy, we are encouraging the rapid expansion of fossil fuel production and use. Billions of dollars are already slated for future investments in Alberta's oil sands, the Arctic, Canada's east coast, and new coal-fired power stations in Alberta.

If we do not dramatically change our course, we will not just increase the likelihood that Canada will have to bear the brunt of future climate change. We also run the risk of missing out on the multiple environmental benefits associated with improved energy efficiency and increased use of renewable energy sources. For example, breaking our addiction to fossil fuels will also help to reduce urban smog, acid rain, and the emissions of a number of toxic pollutants. In addition, it will also help us lessen the wilderness destruction associated with fossil fuel exploration, production, and distribution.

More importantly, however, failure to act could make Canada a non-player in the global energy economy of the twenty-first century. Royal Dutch Shell has estimated that 50% of the world's energy needs will be met by renewable energy in the year 2050. That transformation is already beginning. Global production of wind and solar energy grew at annual rates of more than 20% throughout the 1990s. The fact that renewable energy technologies are decentralized, locally based technologies that create more jobs per dollar invested than conventional energy technologies makes them even more attractive.

Canada still has time to become a global leader in the design and implementation of climate change solutions, but it must act quickly. We should begin by committing now to ratify, by 2002, the Kyoto Protocol to the United Nations Framework Convention on Climate Change. That would require Canada to reduce its greenhouse gas emissions to 6% below 1990 levels in the period 2008 to 2012. In addition, to avoid the trap of waiting too late before acting, Canada should establish its own interim emission reduction target for the year 2005. To meet these targets, Canada will have to abandon its current emphasis on voluntary approaches to address climate change and replace it with a mix of financial incentives and regulatory and voluntary initiatives.

Using the Market to Address Climate Change

To begin with, the federal government needs to put in place a major economic instrument that would discourage production and consumption of greenhouse gas intensive goods and services. One option would be a carbon tax. Virtually every major Western European country (Denmark, Norway, Sweden, Finland, Germany, France, Italy, the Netherlands, and the United Kingdom) has now adjusted energy taxation to ensure that tax levels are more clearly related to the carbon content of energy sources. In most cases, those tax changes were implemented as part of a broader ecological tax reform that saw reductions in other taxes (such as income taxes, payroll taxes, or sales taxes).

Despite considerable public discussion of tax cuts in Canada, there is little talk of tax reform that would increase taxes on things we do not want (such as pollution) and decrease taxes on things that we would like to encourage (such as investment and job creation). While Europeans are moving ahead on ecological tax reform, Canada is standing still. Not only are we failing to adjust market signals to encourage environmental protection, we are missing out on opportunities to reduce other taxes and improve our economic competitiveness. The federal government could take immediate action to ensure that high carbon-content energy sources are taxed relatively more heavily than more climate-friendly energy.

Altering fiscal signals to more clearly encourage the reduction of greenhouse gas emissions is a key element of any credible climate change strategy, but adjustments to the tax system are not the only option. Additional market-based and non-market measures are required. In particular, there is a need to set regulated limits on greenhouse gas emissions from major industrial sources. That should be done through the implementation of a system of domestic tradable emissions permits by the federal government by no later than 2005.

Under a tradable emissions permit system, all major emitters would be required by law to hold permits for their emissions. Only a limited number of permits (equivalent to the environmental objective) would, however, be made available. If an emitter has more emissions than permits, it has two options to comply with the regulation. It could either reduce its own emissions to ensure that it had enough permits to cover emissions or it could purchase additional permits from other emitters.

Emitters will have an incentive to buy permits if they cost less than the price of making equivalent emission reductions internally. Emitters will have an incentive to sell permits if other emitters are willing to purchase them for more than it actually costs to make emission reductions internally. In this way, emissions trading establishes a price for greenhouse gas emissions and creates a market for emission reductions. This market-based solution is more economically efficient than traditional regulation because it provides incentives to find and implement the lowest cost emission reductions instead of simply requiring all polluters to do the same thing. It is environmentally credible because reductions in greenhouse gas emissions will have the same impact no matter where they occur and because accomplishment of the environmental objective is guaranteed by the limit on the number of permits in the system.

Complementary performance-based regulations should also be put in place. Such regulations establish a performance target—such as energy efficiency performance—but do not indicate what specific technologies or processes should be put in place to achieve that objective. For example, the fuel economy of new vehicles in Canada has declined in recent years with the massive influx of SUVs and minivans into the market. The federal government must implement mandatory fuel economy standards that require auto manufacturers to reverse this trend and sharply improve the fuel economy of the vehicle fleet. Such a regulation should seek a minimum 40% improvement in fuel economy by no later than 2008. Manufacturers should, however, have the flexibility to meet those standards in the way they deem most appropriate, which might involve technological changes or changes in the vehicle mix.

There is also a clear need to invest in alternatives to the automobile. The federal government is the only national government within the Organization for Economic Co-operation and Development that does not provide any funding support for public transit. That must change. The federal government must pursue investments in public transit infrastructure and railway networks in much the same way that it supports investments for highways. Such investments must be done in cooperation with provincial and municipal governments and will often need to be accompanied by changes in urban land use planning to be fully effective.

A Green Communities Initiative

While energy efficiency improvements provide both economic benefits—through reduced energy costs, for example—and greenhouse gas emission reductions, many cost-effective opportunities are being ignored because of non-market barriers to investment. For example, many homeowners do not have the information they need to identify energy efficiency opportunities. The federal government should establish a national Green Communities initiative to create community-based organizations that would provide homeowners with an energy audit that identifies the investment costs and energy bill savings associated with potential energy efficiency improvements in the home. Several pilot initiatives in communities across Canada have demonstrated that homeowners will use this information to make cost-effective investments in energy efficiency.

Another barrier to energy efficiency is an inability to obtain financing for capital investments in energy efficiency improvements, even when those investments are cost-effective. The federal government can address that barrier by establishing a "revolving fund" that would provide commercial and institutional building owners with loans that would be repaid from the energy bill savings that result. Such a fund could also provide security for obtaining loans from other institutions. Similar revolving funds have already been piloted very successfully at the municipal level in Canada and now need to be expanded to a national scale.

Last but not least, the federal government must take steps to support the development of a low-impact renewable energy industry in Canada through such sources as wind, solar, biomass, and small hydro. While government intervention of this type is somewhat out of fashion, history shows that the federal government has played a critical role in the development of various energy sources in Canada. Without direct investment from the federal government—as well as loans and loan guarantees, research and development support, and favourable tax treatment—Canada would not have a nuclear energy industry or commercially viable petroleum operations in Alberta's oil sands and off the Newfoundland coast. The federal government must acknowledge that it has an important role to play in facilitating the development of a renewable energy industry in Canada.

A good first step would be to provide financial incentives for both the consumption and production of low-impact renewable energy. Canadians should be provided with a temporary tax credit for the purchase of "green" power. That will help increase the demand for renewable energy and allow producers to obtain economies of scale that can bring costs down. Producers should also be provided with a tax credit tied to production that is guaranteed for a ten-year period. Most industrialized countries have already put in place packages of fiscal and regulatory measures to support the production of low-impact renewable energy. The results are clear: Canada is falling behind.

While the federal government needs to put in place an aggressive package of measures to support the reduction of greenhouse gas emissions and capture the economic benefits that result, it also needs to take other actions in the area of climate change. Continued and expanded investment in climate-change science, technology development, and public education are all important elements of a comprehensive climate change plan.

The federal government will not be able to address the climate change problem on its own. Provincial governments also have a critical role to play in areas such as electricity production, building codes, and waste disposal. Nonetheless, the federal government can, and must, take the first step.

Rick Findlay

Rick Findlay, *is director of Pollution Probe's water program as well as director of its Ottawa office.* In the past, he has been a key player on the climate change issue, in his position with the Global Air Issues Branch of Environment Canada. He was also director of the Ontario Round Table on Environment and Economy, where he led the creation of one of Canada's first sustainable development strategies in that province. His experience also includes being Canada's Niagara River Co-ordinator in the days of Love Canal, and he was a pioneer in waste recycling programs, one of which led to the initiation of the "blue box" recycling system. Mr. Findlay has a degree in chemical engineering from Queen's University.

POLLUTION PROBE
CLEAN AIR CLEAN WATER

63 Sparks Street
Suite 101
Ottawa, Ontario
Canada K1P 5A6
Phone (613) 237-8666
Fax (613) 237-6111

MEMORANDUM

To: **The Prime Minister of Canada**

From: **Rick Findlay** | *Director, Water Program, Pollution Probe*

Subject: **Sustaining Our Clean-Water Heritage**

Abundant, clean water has always been an essential part of the heritage of this wonderful and vast country. Water has provided the pathways by which Canada has been opened up and explored. It supports our agriculture, our industry, and our transportation systems. It supports our economy—it sustains our lives. Water is about life and Canada is about water.

Perhaps you have thought about this as you gazed out over the magnificent confluence of the Ottawa, Gatineau, and Rideau Rivers, from the back door of your home at 24 Sussex Drive. Yet it is amazing to realize that just a few generations ago, our ancestors were able to dip a cup into a river or lake and drink deeply wherever they travelled. The Jesuits, who recognized what a blessed part of the world they were serving, called the Great Lakes the "Sweetwater Seas."

But our magnificent clean-water heritage has almost slipped from our grasp. Canada faces clear problems with our freshwater resources right now—problems of both supply and quality. There are also future threats, in particular from climate change, as well as serious challenges from export and diversion issues as others seek to share our water. In this memo, Prime

Minister, I want to touch briefly on the current problems and future threats—but really to focus on the solutions. I want to tell you what I think needs to be done, by whom, in order to sustain Canada's clean water heritage.

At a global level, water problems are a life-and-death concern in most regions of the world. Tens of thousands of deaths occur every day from water-related diseases, more than from AIDS and cancer combined. Throw in some huge stresses from population growth and some really significant impacts from climate change, and issues of security become a real possibility. After all, clean water is the source of all life, and an adequate supply may be the most precious commodity of all. Wars have been and will be fought over water.

Within Canada, we face a number of problems with water quality. In spite of much good progress, toxic chemicals are a continuing problem, and we are increasingly concerned about certain chemicals that interact with endocrine systems, potentially affecting human growth and development, particularly in children. Lake acidity from acid rain is an issue, particularly in eastern Canada. Contamination of drinking water, particularly from microbiological contamination in the supply systems of small communities and in the north, is now recognized to be a widespread problem, post-Walkerton. Control of surface and groundwater contamination from discharge pipes and "non-point" sources such as agricultural or urban runoff remains a national challenge, and atmospheric pathways now carry persistent toxic substances from all over the world to our lands, lakes, and rivers.

Water quantity issues are significant—even here in Canada, where too few realize that fresh water is a finite and vulnerable national resource. Water scarcity will be one of the consequences of climate change—and evidence of this is already being seen in the Great Lakes, where shipping is being reduced, and in the Prairies, where the agricultural economy needs no further stresses. Water exports are an issue and there is continued uncertainty about the treatment of water as a tradable commodity under the North American Free Trade Agreement.

Abundant cheap energy has also been a huge part of our national heritage. Water and energy are key to life in Canada, in many ways. The international scientific consensus is that global climate change is causing huge changes to the atmosphere and to the endless natural circulation of water between the atmosphere, the land, streams and lakes, and the oceans.

We know we need to reduce emissions of greenhouse gases that are causing climate change, and we know we need to do it urgently. But in the meantime, it is certain that we will also need to adapt to the alterations that climate change will inevitably bring to our ecosystems—and, in particular, our water resources.

Water and energy, then, are connected in many ways. They are the two essential, life-giving, fundamental commodities that beg for your attention and leadership, Prime Minister, as issues that are key to the future of this country.

Sustaining Our Clean-Water Heritage Agenda

So let's now look at a path forward and the elements of the Sustaining Our Clean-Water Heritage agenda you should adopt.

1. TAKE A GLOBAL LEADERSHIP ROLE WITH WATER

The world looks to Canada as a place with huge reserves of clean, safe fresh water and to Canadians as water experts. We will increasingly be looked to for help and we should be able to offer our strengths to the world, not just our water. As Canadians, we should look for ways that we—governments, institutions, businesses, and individuals—can contribute to finding practical, workable solutions to really severe water quality and quantity problems in other countries.

We could focus, for example, on ways that Canada's scientific, technical, institutional, and managerial expertise that has been developed to manage complex, multijurisdictionally administered water bodies such as the Great Lakes might be able to assist other countries facing water crises with their own inland lakes, rivers, seas, and coastal zones. The collaborative Canadian "way of doing business" could be very effective in helping work toward solutions to difficult, seemingly intractable challenges in other countries and cultures. We have developed process skills that may be helpful to others in building their capacity to achieve practical progress.

While global water leadership by Canada should directly serve Canadian interests both environmentally and economically, and from a security point of view, safe and secure water for all is really a matter of ethics and equity. Our future is very much linked to those with whom we share this planet, and the development of a new water ethic should be made a central element of our foreign policy. Adequate clean water should be a fundamental human right, everywhere.

2. DO AN EVEN BETTER JOB OF FIXING THE PROBLEMS WE CAN AND ADAPTING TO THE ONES WE CANNOT

We also have water problems that we need to tackle here at home, and the same new water ethic that should guide our foreign water policy should apply in North America as well. Climate change is altering our continental landscapes and watersheds, right now. Whatever we do to reduce our emissions of greenhouse gases (and we must reduce them a lot!) we must also adapt to the changes that are taking place and that are inevitable.

We must adapt to drought in western Canada, for example, where water systems are already tightly allocated for purposes of drinking water, agriculture, and hydroelectricity. We must adapt to lower water levels in the Great Lakes, and to having less water for navigation and recreation. We must also be ready to help people in other parts of Canada that have increased flood damage, or whose whole ecosystem and way of life is radically changed, as we will find by melting permafrost in our Arctic regions.

The Great Lakes represent an asset that we must manage on a sustainable basis, as a resource of truly national significance. Let's think big and make the Great Lakes the objective of a new, re-energized, bi-national project with the United States. If we focus on what is good for the resource, and what it will take to manage it as an asset on a sustainable basis, we will do the right thing. We cannot afford to do otherwise. Let's really clean up those areas of concern and hot spots of pollution once and for all, and make sure that everyone in North America knows we have a resource we are determined to protect for the long haul.

Turning to the sticky issue of trade and the export of water, we must demonstrate to other North Americans the importance of the Great Lakes and other water systems as essential parts of ecosystems that must be sustained, and as a resource that we value and protect accordingly. Otherwise, we will have difficulty arguing that our water should not be simply another commodity provided to the highest bidder. A good strategy would be to price and manage and conserve our water in knowledge of the full value that it represents, on a sustainable basis.

3. Re-build our capacity to protect our water assets

Our water is a valuable asset that needs to be protected for the long haul. We should take a 100-year view of the future and make decisions about management of our water assets on that basis. We must improve our ability to wisely manage by introducing appropriate laws, regulations, policies and programs. That, in turn, will depend on ensuring effective monitoring, and supporting good science. The capacity to do research is required for the benefit of all, so we have a better understanding of what is going on and why. It means taking a new approach to environmental information and reporting systems, so that we can make the difficult transition from having adequate data to having useful information—and most importantly, to having understanding in every community across Canada.

What greater asset do we have than our health? Safe drinking water is absolutely essential to sustaining healthy people, and the federal government has a vital role to play in helping to provide it. Yes, the provision of drinking water is a matter of strong provincial and territorial responsibilities, but Health Canada has a very important role to play with the provinces in setting health-based water quality standards. It's a unique and important public responsibility that must be enhanced and sustained.

Our country also needs a single, national, comprehensive health-based regulatory scheme for drinking water. Bill C-14, the proposed *Drinking Water Materials Safety Act*, was introduced to the House of Commons in 1997 and was awaiting completion of second reading in 1999, a year before the Walkerton tragedy. It didn't pass, when Parliament was prorogued, but a bill like it should be re-introduced.

A very important factor in providing clean, safe drinking water for Canadians is having high-quality source water to begin with, and here the federal government has a key leadership role to play. Protecting source water means paying more attention to watershed management. We need to take a prevention and protection approach, supporting the continued development and dissemination of ambient water quality objectives, being much more careful about where and how land use and development occur, and about agricultural uses, including livestock operations. Source protection means taking an ecosystem approach—something that is based on the concept of protecting our ecological capital, for the next 100 years.

In summary, Prime Minister, water is a huge part of Canada, and it is time to think big about a new approach to managing it. We need to look upon our water as an asset that must be maintained and protected and sustained, for the long haul. This new approach should be based on a positive, cooperation-oriented, coalition-building model, as opposed to the traditional confrontation model too often applied to environmental issues. The new approach would bring in governments at all levels as well as the corporate community as investors and supporters of progress aiming for continuous improvement. Working together it can happen, but it will take leadership.

However, let's finally be reminded that water is at the heart of a very powerful and emotional connection with Canadians. We have a deeply personal understanding that our clean water is a precious heritage that must be sustained. We know that clean, safe water is central to life itself. Water is essential to our physical survival and water is just as central to our social and cultural lives, especially in Canada—where our whole country is virtually defined by a vast network of waterways. We rejoice in the satisfaction and pleasure, recreation, and renewal that our lakes and rivers provide to us and our families. We cherish our fishing and camping, our chalets and cottages. We are proud and pleased that the rest of the world views Canada as the land of abundant, clean water and we must, therefore, be experts in protecting and managing that water. We need a new water ethic that will be a path not just to survival—but also to continued prosperity.

Laura Jones

Laura Jones, *is director of the Centre for Studies in Risk and Regulation at the Fraser Institute.* She received her B.A. in economics from Mount Holyoke College in Massachusetts and her M.A. in economics from Simon Fraser University in British Columbia. She is the author of *Crying Wolf? Public Policy on Endangered Species in Canada* and co-author of the first and second editions of *Environmental Indicators for Canada and the United States.* She recently edited *Safe Enough? Managing Risk and Regulation,* a Fraser Institute publication.

THE FRASER INSTITUTE

Offering market solutions to public policy problems since 1974.

HEAD OFFICE:
4th Floor, 1770 Burrard Street
Vancouver, British Columbia
Canada V6J 3G7
Phone: (604) 688-0221
Fax: (604) 688-8539
Web site:
   www.fraserinstitute.ca
E-mail:
   info@fraserinstitute.ca

TORONTO OFFICE:
Phone: (416) 363-6575
Fax: (416) 601-7322

OTTAWA OFFICE:
Phone: (603) 565-0468

CALGARY OFFICE:
301 – 815 1st Street S.W.
Calgary, Alberta
Canada T2P 1N3
Phone: (403) 216-7175
Fax: (403) 234-9010

With strategic alliances in 53 countries.

M E M O R A N D U M

To: **The Prime Minister of Canada**

From: **Laura Jones** | *Director*
Centre for Studies in Risk and Regulation, The Fraser Institute

Subject: **A Different Kind of Environmentalist**

I am an environmentalist, which is to say that I enjoy and value nature and believe that it is important to identify and address serious pollution problems. But I am not a typical environmentalist. The assumptions I make about both the causes of environmental degradation and its solutions are fundamentally different from those of what I will call the standard environmentalist model. My beliefs are best characterized as free-market environmentalism. Simply stated, a free-market environmentalist believes that the incentives created by markets will usually do a better job of protecting the environment than government intervention. Standard environmentalists, on the other hand, believe that regulation is a necessary remedy for markets' failure to provide enough environmental amenity. They consider free-market environmentalism an oxymoron. Let me show you why it isn't—and why it is a powerful philosophy for improving our environment.

Economic Growth

A critical difference between standard environmentalists and free-market environmentalists is their view of economic growth. The standard view is that growth is destructive because producing more pollutes more. In a static world, that is true. But the world is dynamic and there are two strong forces that counteract the produce-more-pollute-more effect. First, the increased income that is generated when more goods and services are produced drives a demand for more environmental quality. Once per capita incomes cover basic food and shelter requirements, cleaner air and water become priorities. That explains why some of the richest countries in the world, such as Canada and the United States, are also the cleanest. Second, economic growth stimulates innovation. Since newer technology tends to be both more efficient and cleaner, it improves environmental quality.

Strong evidence supports the idea that those two factors—the impact of income and technological progress—actually dominate the produce-more-pollute-more effect. According to the World Bank, pollution rates from particulate matter and sulphur dioxide begin to fall at per capita incomes of $3,280 U.S. and $3,670 U.S. respectively. Access to safe drinking water and the availability of sanitation improve almost immediately as incomes rise. Another study, by economists Gene Grossman and Alan Krueger, finds that most indicators of pollution start to fall before a country reaches a per capita income of $8,000 U.S.

That explains why North Americans enjoy the luxury of worrying about infinitesimal levels of pesticide residues on our vegetables while in poor countries many people do not have access to safe drinking water and have no option but to use extremely polluting charcoal or cow dung for cooking and heating fuel. To a free-market environmentalist, economic growth is not the enemy of environmental progress but rather the surest way to solve some of the world's worst remaining pollution problems.

A standard environmentalist will disagree with this line of logic. Instead of focusing on the big picture—higher income countries have less pollution—they call our attention to individual examples of the tradeoff between development and environmental quality: the fact that logging, mining, housing developments, and new shopping malls all have impacts on their local environments. Of course they are correct; any human development will have some impact on the environment. But given that humans populate the earth, the choice is not between a pristine environment if economic growth is controlled and a polluted one if it is not. Capitalist economies, which have higher levels of private ownership and tend to experience higher levels of economic growth, will not deliver a pristine environmental utopia with no pollution but they are capable of delivering more environmental amenity than socialist economies. That is the foundation of free-market environmentalism.

Free Trade

As protests against free trade in Seattle in 1999 and in Quebec City in 2001 demonstrate, most standard environmentalists view free trade as part of the problem. In part, that is because free trade increases specialization, which creates economic growth. But as discussed above, this environmental criticism of trade is unwarranted. Growth leads to an increase in income, which in turn creates a demand for more environmental quality. Free trade has another important environmental benefit, however. Trade forces industries to be more competitive than they otherwise might be, which accelerates the adoption of newer, cleaner technology.

Another reason that some standard environmentalists oppose free trade is that they fear trade will cause a degradation of environmental standards as countries are prevented from pursuing their own higher levels of protection. But trade agreements do not prevent countries from protecting their environments. Article XX of the charter of the World Trade Organization clearly states that member countries may impose trade restrictions that are "necessary to protect human, animal, or plant life or health." The only qualification is that such restrictions must be based on sound scientific evidence and must apply to both importers and domestic producers. That qualification is necessary to prevent disguised protectionism.

Finally, standard environmentalists oppose trade because they believe that it allows rich countries to exploit poor ones. In their view, a fixed amount of wealth exists to be divided between countries and if one country gains, another one loses. But that is not how trade works. If it were, why would any developing country agree to trade? Countries that are open to trade, whether rich or poor, tend to grow faster than those that are not because exchanging goods and services allows for specialization. That, in turn, increases productivity and allows citizens to consume a wider variety and greater amount of goods and services than they could without trade. That positive effect of trade holds for all countries, rich and poor.

Property Rights versus Regulation

Free-market environmentalists believe that well-defined property rights are a powerful tool to protect the environment for two reasons. Ownership creates stewardship incentives and gives individuals the power to fight polluters. As free-market environmentalist Jonathon Adler explains, "Even someone indifferent or hostile to environmental protection has an incentive to take environmental concerns into account, because despoiling the resource may reduce its value in the eyes of potential buyers." Private property makes it possible for environmental groups such as the Nature Conservancy and Ducks Unlimited to protect habitat by purchasing land and establishing wildlife preserves.

Perhaps the easiest way to understand the power of property rights is to look at what happens when they are absent. Many fisheries, for example, are treated like common property—fish do not belong to anyone until they are caught. That leads to over-fishing. Although each fisherman would like the fishery to be healthy in the future, the short-term incentives each faces are at odds with this desire. They know that fish they do not catch today will be caught by someone else. Not surprisingly, that has led to the collapse of many fisheries around the world.

The second important feature of ownership is that under common law it gives people the ability to fight polluters through trespass, nuisance, and riparian rights around waterways. Where governments have not usurped those rights with statutes and regulations, they are powerful tools for protecting the environment. In just one of many examples, the Pride of Derby, an English Fishing Club, successfully sued upstream polluters for trespassing against private property.

In contrast to that approach, standard environmentalists put their faith in government regulations and are seldom seen arguing that stronger property rights would constitute an environmental solution. Their approach is widely criticized by free-market environmentalists. As Elizabeth Brubaker explains in her book *Property Rights in the Defence of Nature*, "Many environmental groups prefer regulatory solutions to environmental problems. But regulations are made by remote governments who, driven by the need to create jobs or some undefined 'public good,' are often the least responsible stewards of natural resources. Governments of all political stripes have given us thousands of reasons not to trust them to protect the environment: they've licensed—and bankrolled —polluters, turned forests into wastelands, emptied oceans of fish, and dammed rivers that were once magnificent."

That is not to say that free-market environmentalists do not believe in any regulations. While critics of the free-market environmental approach often accuse them of such an extreme view, free-market environmentalists recognize that governments have a critical role to play in the definition and enforcement of property rights. Regulations may also have a role to play when property rights are as yet difficult or impossible to assign—for example, in the case of air quality.

But beyond the definition and enforcement of property rights, free-market environmentalists view regulations with much suspicion. That is in part because well-intentioned regulations often have unintended effects that undermine the original intent of the regulation. For example, the laws passed in the United States designed to protect species inadvertently created the perverse incentive for landowners to view them as a liability. In extreme circumstances, that led landowners who would have otherwise happily co-existed or even protected endangered species to take measures to eliminate endangered species from their property in order to protect their property values.

The Future of Environmentalism

The debate about how best to protect the environment is only just beginning. As incomes around the world continue to increase, so too will the demand for environmental protection. To date, standard environmental thinking has dominated the debate. But free-market environmentalism is gaining ground. People are beginning to understand that while markets are not perfect, neither are governments. They are beginning to recognize that markets can provide incentives for stewardship. As in other areas, the competition between these two ideologies is not to be feared. It can help generate thoughtful debate about how best to protect the environment.

CONSTITUTIONAL
CANADA

Gordon Gibson

Michel Seymour

John Richards

Part Four

Gordon Gibson

Gordon Gibson *has had a wide-ranging career in business and political affairs.* He has been involved in a number of businesses including pre-fabricated buildings and hotels and real estate development, and has served on the boards of several public companies. After spending four years as an executive and special assistant to Prime Minister Pierre Trudeau, he was elected to the B.C. Legislature in 1974 and served as leader of the British Columbia Liberal Party from 1975 to 1979. Mr. Gibson spent twelve years on the Canada West Council, has been a senior fellow with the Fraser Institute since 1993, and his columns have appeared in the *Globe and Mail* and now in the *National Post*.

CONSTITUTIONAL
CANADA

THE FRASER INSTITUTE

Offering market solutions to public policy problems since 1974.

HEAD OFFICE:
4th Floor, 1770 Burrard Street
Vancouver, British Columbia
Canada V6J 3G7
Phone: (604) 688-0221
Fax: (604) 688-8539
Web site:
  www.fraserinstitute.ca
E-mail:
  info@fraserinstitute.ca

TORONTO OFFICE:
Phone: (416) 363-6575
Fax: (416) 601-7322

OTTAWA OFFICE:
Phone: (603) 565-0468

CALGARY OFFICE:
301 – 815 1st Street S.W.
Calgary, Alberta
Canada T2P 1N3
Phone: (403) 216-7175
Fax: (403) 234-9010

With strategic alliances in 53 countries.

MEMORANDUM

To: **The Prime Minister of Canada**

From: **Gordon Gibson**| *Senior Fellow, The Fraser Institute*

Subject: **Regionalism, the Consitution, and Quebec**

"If it ain't broke, don't fix it." That bit of dubious folk wisdom would see us all still driving around in Henry Ford's Model T, which seldom "broke." Unfortunately, such reasoning remains the approach of the current central government to issues of the federation. The mantra is clear and simple. "Canada is the best country in the world. No big changes. We'll just tackle issues as they arise, one step at a time."

Trouble is, the Model T is creaking and groaning. Yes, there might be a lot more miles in the old gal, but reliability and passenger comfort should count for something too. To wit:

- Canada has a primitive, even pathological version of the British parliamentary system. It amounts to a four-year elected dictatorship by a prime minister with a majority (which our equally primitive electoral system regularly delivers—last time, for example, on the basis of the support of only 41% of those actually voting).

- This system locks whole regions out of effective representation in the government. Any region (such as British Columbia, the west, or Quebec) that has the temerity to vote for the losing party has little clout—at least, little clout absent the threat of separation, a method developed to an art form by Quebec.
- Intergovernmental relations are secretive, fractious, and unbalanced. An excellent example of secretive is that eleven finance ministers made the largest tax hike in Canadian history in a closed meeting that changed the rules on the CPP. Fractious is obvious in every daily newspaper. Unbalanced comes because the central government effectively divides and conquers, particularly by way of its capacity to bribe the six small "client state" provinces by use of its spending power.
- As a result, tax resources are wasted by levels of government fighting each other and bidding for favours. Much of the energy of our leaders is used up on sterile contestation over issues of the federation that do nothing for the citizenry. And calling governments to account is made more difficult.
- Meanwhile, alienation grows in the west and separation refuses to go away in Quebec. In an Ipsos-Reid poll in the spring of 2001, 77% of British Columbians felt ill used by Ottawa. And of course support for the "Yes" in Quebec on the 1995 referendum question has hovered in the 40% to 50% range in succeeding years, with no clear trend.

Some Unpleasant Comparisons

Well, never mind. Let's look at what is important. How has the overall performance of Canada, that "best country in the world,"been?

In a few words, not very good. The decline in our standard of living vis-à-vis the Americans is really quite profound. According to the TD Bank, over the past fifteen years our ratio on that measure has dropped from 86% to 78%, while Ireland has zoomed up from 47% to 76%. (Re-read that sentence, and then send for the Irish prime minister!)

Oh well, the standard rejoinder is that we don't want to be like the United States. Detroit, race riots, all that stuff—not comparable, you know.

Yet my town of Vancouver is very like Seattle. Neither is murder city (though Vancouver has a significantly larger drug problem). The good folks in Washington State have a disposable income per capita—at purchasing power parity, which values our dollar at around 80 cents—of *80% higher than British Columbia*, according to the B.C. Business Council.

Seattle is every bit as liveable as Vancouver. Deduct as much as you want from that income comparison for the need of many Americans to pay for their own medicare and the distortion of the "average" figures by Microsoft millionaires. The comparison is still startling.

Canada is a poorer country because of Ottawa bungling, often in simple-minded pursuit of votes. Regional development strategies where the economics don't work; high taxes to pay for public sector waste and corruption such as the HRDC scandal; human and economic tragedies such as the Aboriginal policies; labour market policies that have been followed by paying people not to work; and financing this by a horrendous debt and a lowering of our international wages via the decline of the loonie—all of this is not good government.

The solution is not rocket science. Over the past century we have learned quite a lot about how economies work, how democracies work, and how human beings respond to incentives. It just hasn't been convenient to the powers that be to apply much of this in Canada.

Others in this volume will have wise advice on specific social and economic policies to make our country a better place. My focus is on process, for from that all else flows.

Process in this context means governance and federalism. The governance side must begin with a subtraction from the powers of the prime minister and a vast addition to those of the ordinary MP. That automatically goes a long distance to handling the problems of regionalism. We in British Columbia do not lack for MPs (though we have somewhat fewer than our fair share). Rather, the problem is that our MPs lack clout. Give them clout and much of the regional problem goes away.

The United States is as vigorously regional a country as Canada, but its representatives and senators have the aforementioned clout. When Representative X from Tallahassee votes on an issue, he or she doesn't care as a first concern what the party thinks. The pertinent question is "What do the folks back home think?"

And every American in addition gets a direct vote for the president. So in two ways, each American really owns a piece of Washington, and they therefore support their town and the Constitution. Can we say that for Ottawa? No. Not in British Columbia, at any rate.

We don't need to adopt the American system, just reform our system.

Re-invigorating Federalism

Now to federalism.

The Europeans have a ten-dollar word—"subsidiarity." The European Union is not in fact the best example of the concept, but the principle is that decisions should be made at the lowest level of authority possessing the requisite knowledge and resources. In the western world, that means most economic decisions are made by individuals and private enterprises interacting through voluntary markets. The private marketplace produces most of our wealth and culture.

But some things are best done collectively, and that moves us into *political markets*. This means governments, and their most basic products are essentially those of order, due process, and security. They also produce the "product" of income redistribution.

Subsidiarity applied to governments means that unless economies of scale argue otherwise, one should prefer local government to provinces, provinces to the central government, and national states to multinational institutions. Each level has its place, but the bias is toward small being more beautiful, if any government can be said to be that.

Now, the result of the subsidiarity principle changes with time and technology. For example, when Canada was founded in 1867 it was an administrative convenience for the Colonial Office (decentralization); a pooling of economies for trade purposes (centralization); a financing unit for the latest technology of rail transportation (centralization); and a convenient focus for a part of the overall Imperial defence and territorial expansion.

The world has changed hugely. Defence considerations are rendered irrelevant by the Pax Americana. The administrative values of decentralization have been recurrently proven as provinces have taken on more and more, and latterly as privatization has proceeded around the world.

Trade is now global, and technology is distributive, meaning that production can be as local as one wishes in most fields given the near-zero cost of moving information and the constantly declining cost of moving goods and services.

All of this has necessary implications for governance in Canada. In applying the principles of subsidiarity, it is true that in some cases the central government should have more power. For example, it should have the right and duty to forbid all barriers to interprovincial trade. It should have the right and duty to monitor provincial performance in various sectors—health, education, and so on—and make comparisons across the country and with best practice around the world. The provinces resist both ideas, but surely governments are to serve the public, not themselves?

But by the same token it is time for the dead hand of the *Canada Health Act* to be removed from the provinces in order that they can practise the sort of innovation and experimentation that led Saskatchewan to develop medicare in the first place. The federal administration of the fishery and of aboriginal affairs has produced economic and human tragedies. The provinces could not possibly do a worse job. Immigration is a shared jurisdiction under our current constitution and that concept should be given life (beyond Quebec, where there is joint control).

In other words, subsidiarity is not a one-way street. But it is now Main Street! And cooperation is essential. In part that is because Canadians hate seeing their governments fight, but in larger part it is because the classic federalism of "watertight compartments" is long gone. The three main levels of government—municipal, provincial, and central—inevitably have an impact on each other, and we need better mechanisms to foster cooperation.

For example, the earlier referenced "hidden level of government" that arises out of federal-provincial relations must be opened up to the sunshine, and the towns and cities let in to the process as well. For now the provinces will insist on remaining the interlocutors for the cities, but to do this legitimately they must form their own intraprovincial mechanisms to bring local government to the table. Municipal governments are, after all, the most trusted level of government, and for good reason—they are more open.

At the federal-provincial level we should replace the nigh-useless Senate with a Council of Ministers that has regular meetings and transparent and accountable practices. Such a body would bring the federal and provincial governments together at regular intervals to discuss issues both of intergovernmental coordination and controversy. Regularity would bring progress—no need for "First Ministers Conferences" invariably called at times of crisis. Canadians prefer boring cooperation.

If this sounds a bit like the European Union, well, maybe the best solution for Canada is somewhere between where we and they are now. We have the superior central Parliament (once it is reformed); they have a better intergovernmental system (which also needs reform).

Interestingly, such a constitutional arrangement—for it would in due course require constitutional amendment— would deal definitively with sovereigntist forces in Quebec and the west. There is no way the current central government would buy into such a solution. But a federal election or two hence, a "new federation" referendum in Quebec or British Columbia hence, and Ottawa might be brought to the table.

In any event, world developments are making governments increasingly subject to the simple and uncontrollable-by-governments decisions of individuals as to where they will live (westward migration), at what and how hard will they work under any given tax regime (the brain drain), and so on. Competition, so long and efficiently at work in free markets, is now at work in the political markets. Governments must adapt or perish. Darwin still applies.

Michel Seymour

Michel Seymour | *is a professor in the department of philosophy at Université de Montréal,* where he teaches contemporary Anglo-American philosophy with a particular interest in the philosophy of language and in political philosophy. He was president of Intellectuels pour la souveraineté from 1996 to 1999 and chair of the Commission on Citizenship for the Bloc Québécois from 2000 to 2001. He has edited three collections of articles on nationalism and has studied the collective rights of people in multination states. Mr. Seymour received his Ph.D. in philosophy at Université du Québec à Trois-Rivières, studied at Oxford University while writing his thesis, and conducted post-doctoral research at UCLA.

Université
de Montréal

Faculté des arts et des sciences
Département de philosophie

C.P. 6128, succursale Centre-ville   Téléphone : (514) 343-6464
Montréal QC H3C 3J7   Télécopieur : (514) 343-7899

M E M O R A N D U M

To: **The Prime Minister of Canada**

From: **Michel Seymour** | *Professor of Philosophy, Université de Montréal*

Subject: **A New Partnership for Quebec and Canada**

The relationship between Quebeckers and Canadians is stuck in a deadlock. The reason is that Canadians want to impose upon Quebeckers two alternative options that they do not accept: the status quo or total independence. Quebeckers are instead favourable to two very different political models: a multinational federation or a confederation of sovereign states (both of which presuppose—and require Canadians to accept—that there is a Quebec people).

I personally believe that a multinational federation is no longer an available political option, and that is why I prefer a confederation of sovereign states. But before presenting that argument, I shall describe what it would mean for Canadians to accept a multinational federation—the ten reforms that are necessary to keep Quebec in a renewed federation.

1. It would mean, first, accepting the need to recognize formally the Quebec people's existence in the Constitution. The Aboriginal peoples are recognized in provisions 25 and 35 of the 1982 Constitution, and there is no reason why Canadians should resist amending the Constitution in a way

that would allow for a formal recognition of the Quebec people. This demand was formulated in the 1960s in the report of the Laurendeau-Dunton Commission.

2. Canadians would also have to accept that the principle of equality of status between the provinces couldn't be applied to Quebec. If national recognition is to mean anything, there should be a special status given to the province of Quebec within the federation. That is a very old demand, probably first formulated in the 1960s by the provincial Liberals.

3. That would in turn entail an acceptance of a general principle of asymmetry in the distribution of powers. Some powers could be offered to the Quebec government without having to offer them to the nine other provinces. Quebec therefore could become more autonomous without weakening the federal government.

   In practice, there is already a certain asymmetry involved in federalism. Quebec is the only province that has its own income tax, its own civil code, its linguistic laws, its own pension plan, and a certain control over immigration policies. The idea is now to accept such asymmetry formally, as a matter of principle, and to increase it in order to meet Quebec's traditional demands. That was a recommendation of the Pepin-Robarts Commission in the 1970s.

4. There should also be a formal recognition that the Quebec government has the responsibility to protect and promote the French language in Quebec, as long as it is done in harmony with the requirement to protect the individual rights of all Quebec citizens and the collective rights of the anglophone community within Quebec (as well as those of the Aboriginal peoples). That was part of the distinct society clause in the Meech Lake Accord.

5. The Quebec government should be the only government responsible for matters related to culture, telecommunications, and the Internet on Quebec's territory. In other words, Quebec should be "sovereign" in matters related to culture.

That was a demand of the late Robert Bourassa in the early 1970s. It was then repeatedly requested by a minister of culture in the Liberal government, Lisa Frulla, and then by all the ministers of culture within Quebec.

It needs to be recognized that there is a national common public culture in Quebec that is very different from the national common public culture in the rest of Canada. The multiculturalism policy of the federal government should be amended so that it becomes clear that the protection and promotion of the language and culture of immigrants has to go hand in hand with their linguistic integration into one of the two welcoming political communities (Quebec and the Rest of Canada).

6. There should also be a limit on the federal government's spending power, which has constantly been a way to intrude in provincial jurisdictions such as education and health programs. Even if, according to the Constitution of 1867, some of these jurisdictions entirely belong to the provinces, the federal government has always used its spending power to increase its presence in provincial affairs. This abusive use of its spending power has been accepted by the Supreme Court. But Quebeckers have always required that the federal government should not use this power to intervene into those jurisdictions. So there should be a formal opting-out clause allowing for financial compensation on any new program implemented by the federal government in Quebec's jurisdictions.

That is a very old request, mentioned in the Meech Lake Accord. It was also a recent request made by the Bouchard government during the negotiations that led to the framework on social union. An opting-out clause for federal spending on shared programs is not enough because, with its actual surpluses, the federal government can very easily respect this last principle and still spend as much as it wants in exclusive provincial jurisdictions, as long as the programs are funded solely by the federal government. The only obligation of the federal government in the framework is to "consult" the provinces beforehand. That is unacceptable. Quebec needs an opting-out clause for all federal programs in Quebec's jurisdictions.

7. Quebec should have a veto over any modification to the Constitution. That was also part of the Meech Lake Accord.

8. A political recognition of Quebec as a nation must also go hand in hand with the recognition that Quebec has a special responsibility toward its national economy. Therefore, Quebec should be afforded all the powers related to unemployment insurance in addition to those concerning manpower training. There is a consensus in Quebec on this issue. It has been there for at least thirty years.

9. Quebec should have the power to appoint three of the nine judges in the Supreme Court. That was also part of the Meech Lake Accord. A true political recognition of the existence of a Quebec people should go hand in hand with appropriate representation. By allowing appointments to be made by Quebec at the level of the Supreme Court, Canada would be showing that it is taking very seriously the fair representation of Quebec within the Canadian constitutional order.

10. Quebec should be allowed to increase its presence on the international scene in its own jurisdictions. That is the Gérin-Lajoie doctrine, again more than three decades old. Quebec should be allowed to participate in international forums on language and culture and should be able to act as an autonomous economic region when Quebec companies are involved. The interests of all the economic regions of Canada should be at the core of the policies defended by the Canadian representatives in international forums such as the World Trade Organization.

Those are ten principles that if agreed to in the past would have reflected the multinational character of Canada, as far as Quebec is concerned. To them I must now add, of course, that the *Clarity Act* should be abrogated because it is anti-democratic and authoritarian in spirit. The Meech Lake Accord was actually a watered-down version of the true historical demands of Quebec. The above principles go to the heart of the matter.

It could be possible to implement these principles without difficulty since they would actually allow business as usual for Canadians even if things were much different for Quebeckers. That's an important point to stress: The daily lives of Canadians would not be changed by these constitutional changes! But for Quebeckers, it would mean that Canada has become a welcoming country for the Quebec people.

There used to be a time when it was said that nothing would please "separatists." That was a comforting thought for Canadians, but also a "slippery slope" argument. It was useful to think that way because it concealed the fundamental inability of Canadians to recognize the existence of a Quebec people.

I realize that many other changes have to be made in Canada beyond those I cite. As far as the Aboriginal populations are concerned, the federal government should apply the main recommendations contained in the final report of the Royal Commission on Aboriginal Peoples. Canada would then not only be a de facto multination state but also truly become a de jure multination state.

There are also changes that have to be made in order to meet the worries of the western provinces. And of course federal institutions also have to be reformed. We need a new electoral system that would incorporate elements of proportional representation. We need a law on private funding for political parties (just like the one in Quebec) and a law on conflicts of interest (just like in Quebec). And the prime minister should not be the one who has all the powers for the nomination of Supreme Court judges, Senators, and other important officials.

Many will want all those changes to be incorporated simultaneously in the Constitution because of the difficulties involved in applying the amending formula individually to each. More likely, we would hear the argument that we must first agree on modifications to the amending formula before making any constitutional change. That would bring us back to square one—the Trudeau legacy.

The Case for Sovereignty and Confederation

Faced with that inevitable blockage, an increasing number of Quebeckers believe that a fast track is available: Quebec should become a sovereign country. That is not like entering a black hole. The complexity of the process would be concentrated in negotiations leading to the transfers of many ministries from the federal government to the Quebec government. Those changes would occur within a period of two or three years, and experts on both sides would settle the matter. For Quebeckers and Canadians, it would be like experiencing a surgical operation.

But Quebec nationalists are responsible people. They also propose partnership links—economical and political—with the Rest of Canada. The partnership offer is not like wanting to have our cake and eat it too. It is an offer that takes into consideration the needs of Canadians for unity. After Quebec has become a country, there could be a strong economic union from coast to coast, with common institutions—a confederation? —whose sole purposes would be to deal with the economic union. Once again, it would not be the end of the world for Canadians. Their federal and provincial governments would still be there, and the additional political structures could be kept to a minimum.

Some Canadians try to ridicule this proposal because a confederation seems to involve a parity of votes for Quebeckers and Canadians. That assumption wrongly presupposes that the council of ministers would have to be composed of representatives of the Quebec government and of the Canadian government. But a variable geometry could be incorporated into the system. On some questions, the council would include only representatives of Canada and Quebec. But on some other matters, there could be also representatives of the Aboriginal peoples.

And on economic issues, there could be representatives of the different regions of Canada. That would partly resolve the alienation of western provinces.

Such a model would be a confederation because all representatives would have a veto. But it would not mean that Quebeckers have parity in our common institutions. I believe, dear Prime Minister, that since Canadians don't believe in a true multinational federation, we should begin the discussions right now on this partnership offer.

John Richards

John Richards | *grew up in Saskatchewan where in the 1970s he served one term as a member of the provincial legislature and of Allan Blakeney's NDP government.* Trained as an economist, he now teaches at Simon Fraser University. He writes extensively for the C.D. Howe Institute, where he holds the Roger Phillips chair in social policy. He frequently teaches in Bangladesh. His latest publication is *Natural Gas Options for Bangladesh*, a co-authored study proposing to use domestic natural gas to accelerate the country's electrification.

CONSTITUTIONAL
CANADA

SIMON FRASER UNIVERSITY

FACULTY OF BUSINESS ADMINISTRATION

8888 UNIVERSITY DRIVE
BURNABY, BRITISH COLUMBIA
CANADA V5A 1S6
Telephone: (604) 291-3708
Fax: (604) 291-4920

MEMORANDUM

To: **The Prime Minister of Canada**

From: **John Richards** | *Professor of Business Administration, Simon Fraser University*

Subject: **Beware Hubris—Be Generous in Victory**

My advice, Prime Minister, is to be generous in victory. I mean by that, view favourably some of the ideas of your opponents about how this country should be run, notably on the tricky, volatile, and important issues of the federal spending power and language in Quebec.

Before I burden you with things to do, my congratulations to the Liberal Party on winning a third consecutive election. I admit that I both underestimated the tactical skill among Liberals and overestimated it among your opponents. Liberal election planners realized—and I didn't—that, without Jean Charest, the Tories had little appeal to francophones and that your party, not the Bloc Québécois, would be the major beneficiary of ex-Tory voters in Quebec. Admittedly, the Bloc is not a spent force: it increased its share of the popular vote between 1997 and 2000. Nonetheless, for the first time, the Liberals bested the Bloc in the province's popular vote. Unless Bernard Landry proves a more skilled politician than either of us believe, you have prevailed over the sovereigntists. Francophone Quebeckers may lack the gung-ho nationalism of the Toronto Star but the majority of them have more or less come to the decision they prefer Canada as it is to the uncertainties of secession.

Let me acknowledge a second conflict that the last election seemingly resolved in your favour. Ever since the NDP's founding convention in 1961, your party and the NDP have vied for the loyalty of that group of Canadians most inclined to favour the welfare state. (A common feature among that group is to want Ottawa to run the show. Ottawa should constrain the "junior governments"—by means of national standards imposed on provincial programs and conditions attached to intergovernmental grants.) Until the 1990s, the NDP enjoyed the support of 15% to 20% in federal elections. In the last three elections, the NDP's popular vote has been cut roughly in half. I doubt the NDP will be able to mount further credible national campaigns. Why? Union leaders will not fund a fourth debacle. Doctrinaire left-wingers will engage in self-delusional rhetoric and claim the NDP could have remained a powerful voice had it been more aggressively radical; most unionists will quietly adopt the American pattern of exercising what influence they can within other parties, including your own.

In part, the Liberal victory over the federal NDP arose because NDP governments in Ontario and British Columbia proved so administratively incompetent. Even the most enthusiastic advocates of an expansive welfare state now balk at the prospect of union-dominated politicians in charge of federal public finances.

There is more to the NDP's demise than falling on its sword, however. I'm thinking of the Liberal government's decision prior to last year's election to roll back much of the 1996 unemployment insurance reform. Most analysts agreed that the 1996 UI reform made sense. The pre-1996 regime was bad for all concerned: it was unduly expensive and, more serious, it contained too many incentives for people in high-unemployment regions to opt for low-skill seasonal work and to avoid training for and migrating to higher-paying jobs in other regions. While good policy, the 1996 reforms was electorally costly: in 1997, the Liberals lost two-thirds of their Atlantic caucus to the NDP and Tories. Rolling back the 1996 reform was bad policy; it was obviously good politics. In November 2000, your party increased its caucus in Atlantic Canada, and thereby humbled both Alexa McDonough and Joe Clark.

You did not push Joe Clark entirely off the electoral stage. He won his Calgary riding and salvaged enough of his caucus—just enough—to remain leader of a recognized political party in Parliament. Clark may be an irritant due to his parliamentary debating skills, but he is no threat to your electoral coalition. If anything, he is an "objective ally" inasmuch as his presence perpetuates division on the political right.

Above all, Liberal election strategists understood how potentially unstable was the rightward-tilted Alliance platform. The one solid plank holding it up was a promise of across-the-board income tax cuts. Via the mini-budget of October 2000, you stole that plank. Thereafter, their platform collapsed.

Let me offer a few words of caution. We in the west disliked your party's demonizing of Stockwell Day as an intolerant Christian fundamentalist. Westerners have a long tradition of supporting religious leaders who abandon the pulpit for politics. That is as true of the left as of the right. The NDP's first federal leader was Saskatchewan's Baptist preacher and patron saint, Tommy Douglas. For many years, Preston Manning's father governed Albertans for six days of the week and preached to them by radio on the seventh. The Saskatchewan NDP early in 2001 chose Lorne Calvert, a United Church minister, as Roy Romanow's replacement and hence premier. Many in the west rallied to the Alliance not out of agreement with their conservatism but out of sympathy for a favourite son whom, we felt, smug easterners were maligning.

All in all, however, Liberals have reason to be proud at winning three straight majorities. Once again, congratulations.

The Next Step

With your opponents bloodied and demoralized, the question arises, what do you intend to do with that victory?

My advice is disarmingly simple: avoid hubris by acknowledging that many of the arguments of your opponents make sense. Somewhat more prosaically, here are two specific suggestions.

1. **Accept a meaningful constraint on exercise of the federal spending power in areas of primary provincial jurisdiction.**

An article of faith among your colleagues is that Ottawa should be able to spend on any matter that Parliament deems appropriate. With all due respect, you are wrong on this. An unconstrained federal spending power ultimately makes a mockery of Canada as a federation. It invites Canadians to lobby both orders of government on all aspects of public policy; it confuses accountability for program outcomes. Canada is "the best country in the world" in part because it has the advantages of a (reasonably) competent central administration plus (reasonably) competent subnational administrations able to innovate in social policy and manage complex programs.

Among the most significant decisions by the Liberal government were those surrounding the 1995 budget. You put an end to two decades of continuous federal deficits and—quite rightly—did so not by further increases in tax rates but by program cuts. Transfers to the provinces were too large and—again quite rightly—you cut them in roughly the same proportion as most other program spending. The jolt of federal "disspending" had a bracing effect on the provinces. For the first time in decades, they collectively thought hard about intergovernmental coordination of budgeting and program design. By 1998, they came up with their so-called provincial consensus document. It called for joint federal-provincial co-decision on new national social programs, a commitment to better outcome evaluation, and a workable constraint on the federal spending power. When the premiers met in Saskatoon in 1998, all ten, including Lucien Bouchard, signed on.

Perhaps the "provincial consensus" was too decentralist a document for your colleagues to abide. But the federal government's response was, I submit, an inelegant counter-reformation. Essentially, you used newfound federal surpluses to bribe most provinces into abandoning their position and threatened recalcitrants with an ideological inquisition: You would accuse them of wanting to gut medicare. The result was the Social Union Framework Agreement, signed in February 1999 by the federal government and all provinces except Quebec. It was an agreement largely tailored to satisfy the federal Liberal agenda. That agenda was not without merit, but it left most of the provincial agenda on the cutting-room floor. The social union agreement is up for review in 2002. Were you to revisit the "provincial consensus," you would achieve several worthy goals.

Almost certainly, you would improve the future coordination of Canadian social programs. Most western Canadians and most francophone Quebeckers favour a fairly decentralized form of federalism. By accommodating some of our agenda, you would also go some way to assuaging western alienation and reconciling Quebec nationalists to a federal future. We may be wrong to resist taking direction from Ottawa, but there it is: It's bred in our jeans.

2. Indicate clearly, in word and deed, that your government believes that "la Loi 101, ça va."

While language policy has divided Canadians for decades, no major challenge to the status quo is under way. Why, to use a double entendre, jab a dormant wasp's nest? Several answers.

First, the nest is dormant only when viewed from "English" Canada; francophone Quebeckers are not dormant. A high-profile commission has recently reviewed the status of French in Quebec. The commission received many submissions, covering many subjects. Some have stressed improvements to the quality of French instruction in schools. Some analyzed and projected the evolution of language use in Montreal, in particular the linguistic choices being made by allophones, those with neither French nor English as mother tongue. Some have argued that extending Bill 101's constraint on English instruction to include the CEGEPs—Quebec's community colleges—is necessary to stabilize language use. On the other hand, certain anglophone organizations have called upon Quebec to abandon any restriction on provision of public services in English and adopt the federal principle of equal treatment for both official languages.

Second, there are pragmatic reasons to do this. You know as well as I that francophone Quebeckers accord a legitimacy to Camille Laurin's Charte de la langue française—or Bill 101—comparable to that granted by the rest of the country to Pierre Trudeau's Charter of Rights and Freedoms. And a plurality of francophone Quebeckers believe the status of French would be more secure were Quebec sovereign. That belief underlies a good deal—not all, but a good deal—of the appeal of secession. Were you to recognize the value of Bill 101 in advancing the public use of French, you would prove the sovereigntists wrong in their claim that only in a sovereign Quebec is defence of French politically secure.

The third and fundamental answer is that Quebec nationalists are right about the case for linguistic protection of French in Quebec. Minority language services matter, and defining them is an important political task. But no country whose *raison d'être* includes survival of more than one language community can rely on Trudeau's mantra: equal treatment across the country for speakers of official languages. All countries in Canada's position—such as Switzerland, Belgium, and India—legitimize versions of Bill 101 whereby local linguistic majorities devise public policies to favour the local majority language over other contenders. India went so far in the 1950s as to redefine state boundaries to correspond to linguistic boundaries. In effect, India's states have enacted over a dozen Bill 101s.

The most convincing argument of the sovereigntists against continued participation in the Canadian federation was always that Charter-based court rulings would progressively undermine the ability of the Quebec Assembly to legislate linguistic protection. Countering that argument will not be easy. Trudeau never allowed doubts about his linguistic mantra. For you to introduce such doubts would be the equivalent of Nixon's going to China. Beyond the matter of breaking with party ideology, MPs representing official language minority ridings comprise perhaps a quarter of your caucus and, given the interests of their constituents, many of them intensely dislike Bill 101. They portray Laurin's Charte as an illegitimate infringement of what the courts should rule to be language rights implicit in Trudeau's Charter.

Ideally, I would like a constitutional amendment acknowledging Laurin right and Trudeau wrong, but that is asking too much. Leave aside entrenchment. More important than any legalities are public attitudes. Persuading your supporters to acknowledge—even in part—provincial arguments over the Social Union Framework Agreement and Quebeckers' case for linguistic protection would do the country good.

I suggest nothing radical, just a little generosity in victory.

CONCLUSION
CONCLUSION

BEYOND WORDS:
THE ROAD TO ACTION

Harvey Schachter

Memos bespeak urgency. Memos bespeak action. They are generally written for limited distribution between colleagues hoping to clarify, promote, and develop consensus.

The memos in this book, on the other hand, are receiving wide, public distribution. The authors are not colleagues of the prime minister—indeed, some of the writers chuckled when they were initially approached about the notion of sending a memo to the prime minister, since they perceive themselves to be opponents of the government in power. And, of course, the prime minister is not really the prime recipient for the memos in this book, although it would be lovely if he read them and acted upon them. The memos are written for the general public, to clarify, promote, and develop consensus.

We live in an era where it is sometime difficult to tell the difference between utopian ideas and practical ideas. After all, technological miracles abound, and for all the stickiness involved in getting political change, we have seen profound transformations on many fronts in the past few decades. Is it utopian or is it realistic to talk about a clean-water policy for Canada? Is it utopian or is it realistic to promote changes in the way Canada is governed by a small group in Ottawa, and to demand some Parliamentary reform after years of promises from politicians? Is it utopian or is it realistic to consider developing a housing policy to combat homelessness? Is it utopian or is it realistic to suggest making Canada a leader in technology, or to call for significant progress in retarding climate change, or to want a top-quality health system?

In some ways, the ideas our writers present are indeed utopian—too much to hope for. But in many ways, their agendas are eminently practical. The memos often cite other countries that have made the changes proposed. Is it utopian, for example, to adopt social measures that have proven effective in Europe, as several writers urge?

As well, the memos are not written with the expectation of immediate perfection, but with the recognition that political change is a process. And even if the proposals *are* utopian, that doesn't mean they can't stake out worthwhile goals for action. As Hugh Segal notes in his memo, "It may be impossible to eradicate poverty, but it is never wrong to try."

There's a standard program for change in organizations these days. You develop ideas. You set goals and a strategy. You agree on tactics to accomplish your goals. Then you implement, evaluate progress along the way, and make adjustments that will lead you closer to your goal. The process is no different in government, although it can be messier.

These memos demonstrate the first three steps in the process. They present worthy ideas (although as with all brainstorming, some are contradictory, and leaders must choose between them or find an integrative solution that combines the best elements of competing notions). The memos certainly present goals and recommended strategies. Some of the memos also outline tactics for achieving the goals.

The next steps are beyond the scope of this book. They rest with readers, who can push anew for their favourite ideas to be implemented, as well as the prime minister and his colleagues both in Ottawa and other governments across the country, who can take action, evaluate progress, and re-set their course as m o re is learned. Although the ideas in the book build a formi-da ble agenda, the prime minister has a cabinet with ministers re s ponsible for the various issues tackled in this book, who in tu rn have a legion of staff to implement them. Politics is the art of the possible. And most of these ideas are possible, if our gov-er n ment and citizenry are willing to adopt some stretch goals.

Memos bespeak urgency. Memos bespeak action. It is ho ped that these memos will be of more than intellectual inter-es t, but that in some way they can contribute to action that im prove this country.

CREDITS

CREDITS

PHOTO CREDITS

Gail Bowen, photograph by Don Hall.

Jason Clemens, photograph courtesy of The Fraser Institute.

Raisa Deber, photograph courtesy of the Faculty of Medicine, University of Toronto.

Joel Emes, photograph courtesy of The Fraser Institute.

Peter Holle, photograph courtesy of *Winnipeg Free Press*.

Robert Hornung, photograph by Ellen Burack.

Laura Jones, photograph by CP Foto and Frame.

Stephen Lewis, photograph courtesy of the Canadian Institute of Research (Ottawa).

Margaret Little, photograph by Bernard Clark.

John Loxley, photograph by Liberty Studios Ltd.

Roger Martin, photograph by Jim Allen.

Fred McMahon, photograph courtesy of The Fraser Institute.

Matthew Mendelsohn, photograph by Classic Photography (Toronto).

Bruce O'Hara, photograph by Ian Robbins.

Nancy Olivieri, photograph courtesy of *Maclean's Magazine* (1998).

David Pecaut, photograph by Andrew Kolb.

Bob Rae, photograph courtesy of BGM Imaging.

John Richards, photograph by Bayne Stanley.

Donald J. Savoie, photograph by Photographie Maillet.

Hugh Segal, photograph by Wanda Goodwin.

Michel Seymour, photograph by Geneviève Sicotte.

Sheelagh Whittaker, photograph courtesy of EDS Canada/Susan Cornell.